D1611490

SEW FOR YOURSELF

SEW FOR YOURSELF

50 Great Garments from Recycled Fabric, Using 5 Basic Patterns

Ingrid Bergtun
Ingrid Vik Lysne

SCHIFFER
CRAFT

4880 Lower Valley Road • Atglen, PA 19310

About the Garments in This Book

Ingrid Pants

It can be difficult to find the perfect pants when shopping. In this chapter, we show you how you can make your own pants to fit your body. We offer four different pants patterns: pants with straight legs, flare pants, slacks, and cargo pants.

Dresses

This chapter features shirt dresses, dresses with gathers, and with long or short sleeves. The dresses can be sewn for both summer and winter depending on what type of fabric you choose. In addition, we show you how to make a special festive dress (sharing a bit of lovely tradition from Norway, our home) and how you can revamp a dress you already have into a ball gown.

Tops

In this chapter, you'll find everything from simple T-shirts to tops and pullovers with round necks, a hood, or collar. In some of the patterns, you should follow the instructions exactly. In others, we show you how you can make adjustments, so, for example, regular sleeves can be transformed into puff sleeves.

Ingrid Jacket

All the jackets in the book begin with the same basic pattern: the Ingrid jacket. If you sew one from a blanket, you can make a super autumn jacket. We'll show you how to make a raincoat with waterproof fabric, and a puffy jacket using an old comforter.

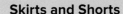

Skirts and Shorts
In this chapter you'll find patterns for various styles of shorts, a carpenter jumper, a summer skirt, and skirts to wear in colder weather. All the skirts begin with your own measurements to fit your body perfectly.

Jumpsuit
This chapter teaches you how to make a jumpsuit from scratch, how to make a jumpsuit out of a dress, and how to sew a jogging outfit. These can all be made fancier or as comfortable garments for relaxing.

Fabric Remnants
All the patterns we designed in this chapter are perfect for using up fabric remnants. Some need only small pieces, others a bit more. You can sew scrunchies, makeup pads, bucket hats, and caps.

Bags
This chapter is full of patterns for bags: tote bags, coin purses, and fanny packs, all of which are fine accessories to go with the other garments in this book.

Redesign and Repairs
Here you'll learn simple methods for redesigning and repairing garments. If, for example, you find a hole in a top, you can embroider over it or sew on a patch and embellish it with beads. Redesigning is often easier than sewing from scratch since you can usually retain many of the details of the original garment.

Ingrid Shirt
This shirt design works for both men and women. It has a straight silhouette and can be shortened or lengthened as necessary. Sew it in cotton for a traditional look or finer fabric if you want a lighter shirt. It can also be worn as a jacket if you make it in a heavier, sturdier fabric.

Contents

See the inside pocket for the 5 Basic Patterns, customizable to all sizes

Our Sewing History

The idea behind this book was to show not only that it's possible to make your own clothing, but that it's also easy and fun, and, not least, sustainable. You don't need a lot of fancy tools or training to begin to sew. As long as you have a sewing machine, you are ready to go. The best method of learning how to sew is through trial and error. Tip number one for understanding how clothes are put together: take a look at some of your own clothes.

We're both self-taught but learned to sew in different ways. Ingrid B began sewing only four years ago. She was greatly inspired by discovering that it's possible to make clothing just as nice as what's found in shops. In the beginning, she followed patterns step by step and googled every word, and, after that, she had a greater understanding of the subject. She began to try out her own ideas and used, as a starting point, the garments she had in her wardrobe to make new ones.

Ingrid VL began sewing when she was 10 years old. She sewed teddy bears and redesigned her clothes. She found pleasure in designing and in teaching herself everything. She wanted to have complete creative freedom and never follow patterns. It took a long time when she had to discover everything herself, but, at the same time, she became especially good at thinking outside the box, finding new solutions, and transforming her own ideas into garments.

Ingrid B wanted to learn how to sew so she could make garments as nice as those in the shops. Ingrid VL began sewing to make garments she couldn't find in the shops. We hope everyone who reads this book will be as happy with sewing as we are. Good luck!

Ingrid Vik Lysne & Ingrid Bergtun

How to Use This Book

The goal of this book is to be so easy that new beginners will understand the patterns, but, at the same time, to be so inspiring and educational that even those who have sewn for many years will find pleasure in it. Some of the patterns are harder than others. We recommend that you look over the instructions before you begin so you'll have an overview of what is involved, and can decide if the difficulty level is appropriate for you.

For some of the patterns, you cut out the pieces following a template, and for others, you'll draft the pieces yourself from your own measurements. Some of the patterns use elements from other designs as a starting point. For example, the pants and pullover patterns are also used to make a jumpsuit.

We each sew a bit differently and have developed our own methods based on how we learned. There are many ways to produce finished garments, and we want you to feel free to make things in your own way. Because we each sew differently, you'll find that some things vary in the book. Ingrid VL likes, for example, to zigzag or overlock all the pieces first, but Ingrid B likes to do this as she goes along.

There are many techniques that reappear in the various patterns. We gathered these related explanations into their own chapter. We haven't always fully written out some steps in the process—if it is a step that's regularly repeated, such as, for example, pinning the fabric before seaming, and pressing seamlines open when you've sewn them.

Throughout, we've been inspired and learned so much through social media. You can ask questions concerning patterns, share pictures, and see how others have sewn their garments. We are always so excited to see what is made from our patterns! Please search us out on social media.

HOW MUCH FABRIC DO I NEED?

When you're sewing with recycled textiles, you cannot chose how much fabric is available. You most often have to suit the garment to the fabric; for example, by making a skirt a little shorter or having fewer ruffles on a dress. For that reason, we have not included the number of yards or meters of fabric you'll need for each pattern. To find out if you have enough fabric, lay out all the pattern pieces on the fabric. Don't forget that some pieces may be cut out several times. Pattern placement and cutting out is a little puzzle that we immensely enjoy. If you are going to go out and buy new fabric and wonder how much you'll need, you can lay out all the pattern pieces on some fabric you already have, such as a comforter cover or sheet.

HOW TO USE THE PATTERNS IN THIS BOOK

The measurements you cut out the fabric pieces from are the *pattern*. This book has pattern instructions, for which you cut out following a pattern; it also has instructions for cutting out the pieces based on your own measurements.

You'll find the paper patterns inside this book's cover. The lines for the various sizes are superimposed one above the other. Unfold the sheet and trace the pattern you need; for example, on a blank pattern sheet or tracing paper. On the next page, we'll teach you how to fit the pattern to your measurements if you are between sizes. All the patterns include a ⅜ in (1 cm) seam allowance, which means that you will cut out the fabric edge to edge with the pattern and sew ⅜ in (1 cm) inside the fabric edge.

Don't forget to include all the markings (for example, for darts and tucks) when you trace the pattern. The arrows on each of the pattern pieces show the direction of the fabric threads. On the sleeves, two lines indicate the back and one line is for the front. You'll see the same on the front and back. *Cut on fold* means you should fold the fabric and cut out two matching pieces joined across the width.

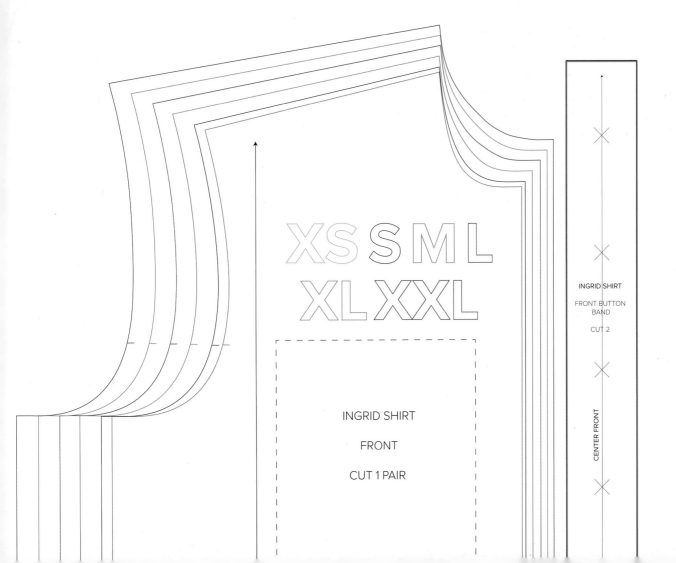

XS S M L
XL XXL

INGRID SHIRT

FRONT

CUT 1 PAIR

INGRID SHIRT

FRONT BUTTON BAND

CUT 2

CENTER FRONT

HOW TO ADJUST THE PATTERNS TO FIT YOU

All bodies are different, and one of the most fantastic things about sewing for yourself is that you can make clothes to fit your body perfectly. You can make some adjustments as you work by trying on the garment and adjusting your stitching. You might make other adjustments when cutting out the fabric. Here is how to adjust the pattern before you cut the fabric.

Step 1: Measure your body. Compare your measurements with those in our table below. Draw a circle around the size closest to your measurements. In this example, we began with the pants pattern to fit a person with a hip measurement closest to size XL but waist size L.

Step 2: Our patterns are distinguished by sizes. If your hip measurement is XL and waist is L, mark one point on the hip line for size XL and a point at the top of the pattern for size L, as shown in the drawings on the next page.

Step 3: Draw a line following the pattern shape between the two points so that you get a new pattern for pants in size XL at the hips and size L at the waist. Then cut out a waistband in size L.

Even if you have made adjustments, you should try on the garment and make further adjustments as you work to make sure that the garment will fit well.

Size	XS	S	M	L	XL	XXL	
Chest	81	85	93	99	109	117	cm
	32	33½	36¾	39	43	46	in
Waist	68	72	80	88	96	104	cm
	26¾	28¼	31½	34¾	37¾	41	in
Hip	91	95	103	111	119	127	cm
	36	37½	40½	43¾	47	50	in
Crotch Length	82	82	82	82	82	82	cm
	32¼	32¼	32¼	32¼	32¼	32¼	in

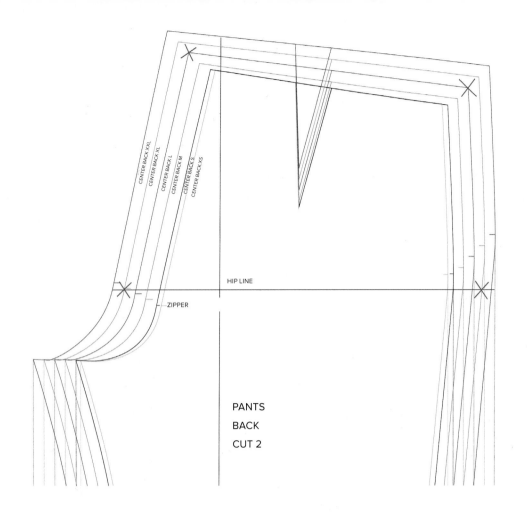

CENTER BACK XXL
CENTER BACK XL
CENTER BACK L
CENTER BACK M
CENTER BACK S
CENTER BACK XS

HIP LINE

ZIPPER

PANTS
BACK
CUT 2

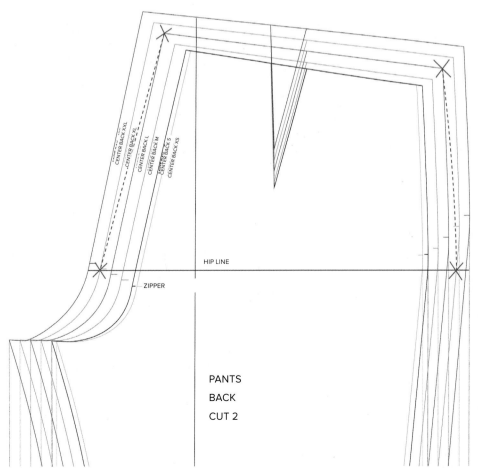

CENTER BACK XXL
CENTER BACK XL
CENTER BACK L
CENTER BACK M
CENTER BACK S
CENTER BACK XS

HIP LINE

ZIPPER

PANTS
BACK
CUT 2

SEWING TERMS

Back = back of the garment

Bias tape = a band cut on the bias of fabric; this makes the band flexible so it can be used around curved and straight edges

Button band = a strip at center front of a shirt where the buttons and buttonholes are placed

Crotch length = length from the crotch to the ground, along inner leg

Cuff = a piece sewn on lower edge of sleeve on simple garments; for example, shirts

Dart = a fold in the garment to be sewn down; used to create shaping in, for example, pants

Front = front of the garment

Gather = a technique for gathering and drawing in fabric

Grommet = a metal ring placed on fabric, usually together with a cord

Hem = where the edge of the fabric is folded up toward the back and sewn down, such as, for example, at lower edges of pants and skirts

Hip measurement = the circumference of hip measurement at widest point

Interfacing = fusible material that can be ironed onto the back of fabric to stiffen it

Overlock = a sewing machine used to sew along raw edges to prevent fabric from unraveling

Pattern = the template one uses to cut out the fabric pieces

Press = press with an iron

Raw edge = the cut edges of the fabric; zigzag stitch along this edge to prevent fabric from unraveling

Seam allowance = the distance between the seam and the raw edge of the fabric

Thread direction = the direction of the fabric follows the selvedge (the selvedges are the two sides of the fabric that won't unravel because they are not cut off)

Top stitching = visible seaming

Tuck = a fold in the fabric sewn down on the edge of the fabric; used to create shaping

Waistband = a piece of fabric to shape the waist on simple pants and skirts

Waist measurement = circumference around waist at smallest

Zipper, invisible = a zipper that cannot be seen on the outside of the garment

Zipper, visible = a zipper with the band and teeth visible showing on the outside side of the garment

Zigzag = stitching along raw edges to prevent fabric from unraveling

Recycled Textiles

For this book, we decided to make all the garments with recycled textiles. There are so many already-produced textiles out there, and we want you to see how many possibilities they offer.

WHY SEW WITH RECYCLED MATERIALS?

Recycling is the thread tying together this whole book. Here's why:

In your country, the situation is probably similar to our own: in Norway, Frentex (Salvation Army) alone takes in 50 tons of textiles every single day. That is so much more than their shops can manage to sell, and as a result, much of what is donated is shipped to sell in other countries. That causes a new set of problems. Several African countries have passed laws forbidding the sale of used clothing from the West because it suffocates the local clothing production and value creation. Textiles that no one wants to have create a big waste problem, one that has increased as clothing has become cheaper.

Sewing with recycled textiles has many environmental advantages. As the textile industry exists today, all new production damages or strains the environment. Cotton production, for example, requires enormous amounts of water; the chemicals used for dyeing and processing are drained into our rivers; and polyester garments shed microplastics when worn and washed. When you use textiles that have already been produced, you contribute to a lower demand for new textiles. In addition, you save textiles from becoming waste.

In addition to sustainability, there are many other advantages to sewing with recycled textiles. You can, for example, sew one-of-a-kind garments, fashion that no one else will have. If you have textiles with a sentimental value, such as your grandmother's tablecloths or the old kitchen curtains from your home, you can restore them as garments so the textiles will continue living with you. Also, you can make super exclusive garments for little money. Used hand-embroidered cloths that took months to embroider and exclusive brocade fabrics are often sold at a fraction of the price you would have paid if you bought them new. Some textiles become even better with time. Good used sheeting can, for example, be much softer than new.

HOW TO SEW WITH RECYCLED MATERIALS

Sewing with recycled textiles takes a bit more thought than sewing with newly purchased fabric. By using new textiles, you might begin with an idea for a garment and buy everything necessary for sewing that garment. With recycled textiles, the process is often the opposite. You find a fantastic piece of cloth and then design a garment suited to that fabric.

If the textile has a lovely print or some details you want to highlight, you should plan before you start cutting. We tend to lay out the pattern pieces on the textile first—and see how it would look, for example, with some embroidered flowers on the shoulders—and then cut out after all the pieces have been arranged. We sometimes use this part of the process if the textiles have elements we want to enjoy. We are first and foremost concerned with placement and the result. The thread direction and rules come in another sequence.

You may not always know what the recycled textiles are made of. Maybe the writing on the tag has disappeared or the textile was hand-sewn. Our best tip for next-to-skin garments is to feel the fabric to find out if it is soft enough. If you want to make an outer jacket, it is more important that the fabric be thick enough so it won't be too slack. Feel the textile and see how it drapes before you decide what you'll make with it.

Curtains and tablecloths are made for interior furnishing use, not for next to the body. For that reason, you need to see and feel the fabric before you decide what to make. Heavy, smooth curtains might perhaps be softened in the washing machine. They might be better for a skirt than a tight-fitting blouse that has to be washed often to remove sweat. Many curtains and other recycled textiles are made with versatile fibers such as linen and cotton, and these are as good on the body as in the home.

We think that sewing with recycled textiles makes anyone even more creative. Sometimes, you might end up making shorter pants than originally intended; other times, you might need to combine several pieces of fabrics to have enough for that dress you are longing to make. This makes the process more exciting, and sometimes the end result is totally different from what you had in mind.

HOW TO SOURCE RECYCLED MATERIALS

When you are going to sew with recycled textiles, you have to think differently than when you are going to use newly purchased fabric. Fabric stores have a huge selection, so you should usually go there with a plan in mind and find just the fabric you are after. When buying used, you never know what you will find, and you can't count on what textiles will still be available if you come back a week later. As a general rule, buy the to-be-upcycled textile first, spontaneously, and then think about how you will use it.

TIPS FOR HOW TO SOURCE RECYCLED TEXTILES

- Recycling centers. Not all recycling centers have textiles, but go in anyway. You might suddenly see a fantastic cloth hanging over a chair at the back of the shop.
- Always swing into any shop you come to that has a sign announcing "antiques" or "used."
- Check out flea markets. Look through everything. You might spot a treasure among the torn gloves and gym socks.
- If you are searching for something specific, check online spots where people sell things, such as Facebook Marketplace. You can also search social media friend groups.
- Join buy-and-sell groups on Facebook.
- Ask family, friends, or colleagues about old textiles they want to get rid of.
- Shout out that you are interested in recycled textiles. It may seems a little odd, but write a note and put it in the mailbox of a neighbor or two, if you want to be in contact just in case they have some textiles to get rid of. Why not? Once people know that you are interested in sewing and recycling, they'll think of you when they empty their cupboards.

INGRID PANTS

It can be hard to find the perfect pair of pants in the shops. In this chapter, we'll show you how to make your own pants. We have designed four different styles of pants, which can be varied endlessly when sewn in different textiles. Our pattern will guide you through making straight pants, flare pants, and slacks. All of them have the same basic pattern and are sewn the same way. The flare pants pattern is a complete explanation of how the pants are sewn, and can be used for all the types of pants.

Pattern Sheets: You'll find the pattern for the pants in the pattern sheets in one of the inside cover pockets. All the patterns consist of a front, back, waistband, and two pocket pieces.

Fabric: Pants can be sewn in a variety of fabrics, but we do not recommend the thinnest fabrics, unless you want to have rather loose and drapey pants. We have sewn pants in this book with heavy fabrics, curtains, corduroy, and linen.

Additional Materials: interfacing, regular zipper 8 in (20 cm) or invisible zipper 10 in (25 cm)

Before You Begin: Read the information about how to adjust the fit on pants on page 12. All the pants have a zipper on the back, and you can choose the style of zipper you prefer. "Invisible zipper" is explained on the flare pants pattern. "Visible zipper" is explained on page 26. Don't forget to mark the darts. Press each seam open after sewing it.

Flare Pants

1 Cut out all the pieces, and iron interfacing onto the waistband. Zigzag or overlock around all the edges except for the waistband.

2 Sew the darts on the back pieces.

3 Sew front pocket piece to the front with right sides facing. Press seam open. Fold pocket to back and press. From the front, top stitch along the curve ¼ in (0.5 cm) in from edge, through all layers.

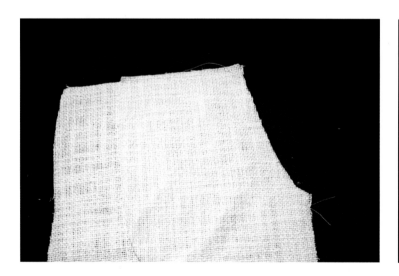

Pattern pieces:

FRONT, FLARE PANTS × 2

BACK, FLARE PANTS × 2

WAISTBAND × 2

POCKET FRONT × 2

POCKET BACK × 2

4 Lay back pocket piece over front piece and sew a seam along curve. You can choose the type of seam to go through all three layers with a visible seam on the front of the pants, or only the pocket lining. Sew the pocket securely to the pants along the top edge and the side (stitch inside the seam allowance so it won't be visible when the waistband and side seams are sewn).

5 With right sides together, sew side seams on both pant legs.

6 With right sides together, sew crotch seam on front.

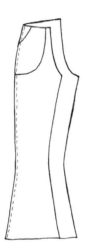

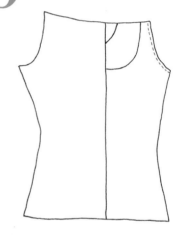

7 Lay waistband with right sides facing and seam along top edge (the top edge dips in). Press seam open, fold band with wrong sides together and press.

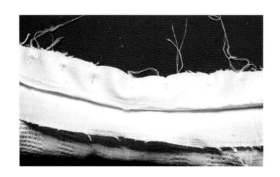

8 Sew one side of waistband to front of pants with right sides facing. Press seam open toward band.

9 Here's how to set in an invisible zipper on center back of pants. Mark top of zipper with two pins, then place two pins 2 in (5 cm) from lower edge. Pin one side of the zipper to the pants, all the way up to fold in waistband. Stitch as close to the zipper teeth as possible without sewing over them. Stop when you come to the pin indicating that 2 in (5 cm) remain on the zipper. Make sure the zipper is invisible and engaging by closing it up. If it isn't invisible, you can stitch closer to the zipper teeth. Pin the other side and attach the same way.

10 Stitch the curve below the zipper. Make sure the seams meet when zipper is closed.

11 Stitch between the legs from one leg to the other, with right sides facing. Make sure that the crotch seams are centered and align.

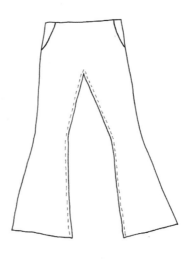

12 Fold raw edges of waistband in ⅜ in (1 cm), press, and pin it to inside of pants. If you stitch from the right side, you'll have more control for a nicer look. Make sure you stitch through all the layers.

13 Fold pant legs up and sew down. You can also fold the edge double.

Straight-Leg Pants

Pattern Pieces:

FRONT, REGULAR x 2

BACK, REGULAR x 2

WAISTBAND x 2

POCKET FRONT x 2

POCKET BACK x 2

Slacks

Pattern Pieces:

FRONT, SLACKS x 2

BACK, SLACKS x 2

WAISTBAND x 2

POCKET
FRONT x 2

POCKET
BACK x 2

Visible Zipper

A visible zipper can be sewn in in several ways. Here is a simple method: change to the zipper foot on your sewing machine. Pin one side of the zipper with zipper and pants right sides facing, all the way up to the folded waistband. You can decide how much of the zipper tape you want showing and how close to the teeth to sew. Stitch from the top down to the bottom stop. When you reach the retaining box, lift the machine foot and pull the box underneath. Sew down the other side of the zipper the same way.

Cargo Pants

Cargo pants are assembled just as for flare pants through step 5. Then follow these steps for making the cargo pockets.

1 Place pocket flaps with right side facing. Stitch along all the edges, except for the top edge. Cut the corners about 1/32 in (1 mm) from the seam, turn and press. On the front, stitch through both layers 1/4 in (0.5 cm) in from the edge.

2 Now make the tucks on the pockets. Fold in two tucks 3/4 in (2 cm), so they meet each other in the center.

3 Fold top edge of pocket 5/8 in (1.5 cm) down to wrong side and sew down. Fold the other side in 3/8 in (1 cm) and press.

4 Try on the pants to make sure they fit, and pin on the pockets where you want them. I placed the pockets 6 1/4 in (16 cm) below the visible seam at the side pockets, and 3/4 in (2 cm) inside side seam of pants. Sew the pockets into place with a visible seam along all sides except for the top.

5 Lay pocket flap ⅝ in (1.5 cm) from pocket opening so that the tip points up. Sew down along cut edges. Trim seam to about ¼ in (0.5 cm). Fold flap down toward pocket, press and stitch about ¼ in (0.5 cm) from top edge.

Continue, following instructions for flare pants on page 20 until finished.

Pattern Pieces:

FRONT REGULAR x 2

BACK REGULAR x 2

WAISTBAND x 2

POCKET
FRONT x 2

INGRID JACKET
POCKET FLAP x 4

POCKET
BACK x 2

INGRID JACKET
POCKET x 4

Tops

Welcome to our tops! In this chapter, you'll find easy T-shirts; pull-overs with round necks, collars, or a hood; decorated tops with flounces; and tops with puff sleeves. You can sew tops with all sorts of recycled textiles, such as tablecloths, curtains, sheeting, or blankets, but we recommend using fabric that's not too heavy or thick. Tops can get sweaty, and they need to be washed fairly often. So we recommend sewing with fabrics that breathe, are comfortable to wear, and are washable.

All the tops are cut out following a pattern. For some of the patterns, you will need to follow the instructions exactly. In others, we will show you how to made adjustments, so you can, for example, change regular sleeves to puff sleeves. None of the tops are close-fitting, but we recommend that you read page 12 to learn about modifying the pattern to fit your body perfectly.

Pullover

Pattern Sheets: Ingrid Pullover

Fabric: This pullover can be sewn with a variety of fabrics, from the lightest curtains to stretch and firm cotton, or a thin wool blanket, as we have done

Additional Materials: bias tape

Before You Begin: Don't forget that the sleeves must be cut out mirror image, and it is a good idea to mark the tucks on the sleeves when you cut them out.

Pattern Pieces:

FRONT x 1　SLEEVE x 2　BACK x 1

CUFF x 2

1 Cut out all the pieces for the pattern and bias tape for the neck. Zigzag or overlock all the edges except for those on the bias tape and cuffs.

2 Cut out all the pieces for the pattern and bias tape for the neck. Zigzag or overlock all the edges except for those on the bias tape and cuffs.

3 Measure the circumference around the neck. Ring neckline with bias tape and sew on (see page 230 for more detailed instructions).

4 With right sides facing, pin sleeves in armholes. We think it is easiest to begin at the center of underarm and the two sides. Then pin the rest and ease in until even. Sew armhole seam.

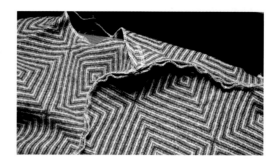

5 Fold in tucks and sew at seam allowance. Place cuffs right sides facing at lower edges of sleeves and sew on. Press seams toward cuffs.

6 Sew each side seam from cuff to lower edge of body. Make sure the underarm seams align.

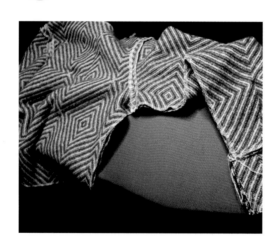

7 Fold the end of the cuff toward the back and sew down. You will have more control if you stitch from the right side—just make sure you sew through all the layers.

8 Finally, hem the lower edge of pullover by folding the edge to the wrong side and sewing it down. You can also fold the hem double if you want.

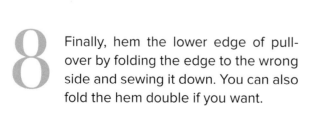

T-shirt

Pattern Sheets: Ingrid Pullover

Fabric: The T-shirt shown here was made from an embroidered cloth. When sewing with embroidered fabric, first consider how to place the motifs. You'll find more about that on page 11. We recommend light fabrics, such as sheeting and thin curtains, or stretchy fabric. But anything goes, and we also often dream about, and sew up, linen T-shirts or party T-shirts made from heavy, smooth curtains.

Additional Materials: bias tape

Before You Begin: You can decide how long you want the T-shirt to be. Some of our test sewists thought it was a bit too short, while others wanted to make it even shorter. For this example, we shortened it on front and back by about ¾ in (2 cm).

Pattern Pieces:

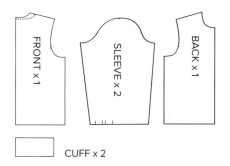

FRONT x 1   SLEEVE x 2   BACK x 1

CUFF x 2

1   Cut out the back and front. Shorten sleeves so they are 7½ in (19 cm) from the top center point and down. We made our T-shirt a little shorter (17¾ in [45 cm] from the neckline down) because the cloth wasn't big enough. Set aside enough fabric to make a bias tape. Zigzag or overlock along all edges.

2   Place front and back with right sides facing and seam shoulders.

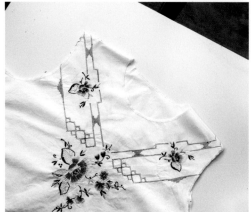

3 Pin sleeves into armholes with right sides facing. We think it is easiest to begin at the center of underarm and the two sides. Then pin the rest and ease in until even. Sew armhole seam.

4 Sew each side seam from outer edge of sleeve to lower edge of T-shirt.

5 Fold the lower edge of body and each sleeve to wrong side and sew down. You can fold a doubled hem if you prefer.

6 Measure the circumference around the neck. Cut and sew bias tape around neck (see page 230 for more detailed instructions).

Sporty Pullover

Sporty might not be the first description that comes to mind for old curtains. However, curtains can definitely become sporty if you add a hood, zipper, and front pockets. You can sew this jacket with a collar or a hood. We made ours entirely following a pattern, but you are free to add grommets and drawstrings, or trim the lower edge with knitting or ribbing. Our jackets were sewn from curtains with embroidered leaves, a sheet, and a silver curtain. You can make these in almost any fabric, but they will drape better with a slightly heavy fabric—perhaps a cotton cloth. They would also work well as an exercise jacket in a sportier fabric or stretch material.

With a Collar

Pattern Sheets: Ingrid Pullover

Additional Materials: zipper, 11–12 in (28–30 cm), interfacing

Before You Begin: Don't forget that the sleeves must be cut out mirror image, and it is a good idea to mark the tucks on the lower sleeves when you cut them out.

Pattern Pieces:

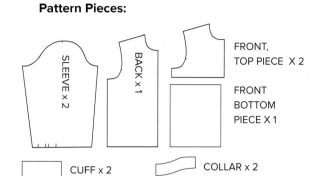

SLEEVE x 2

BACK x 1

FRONT, TOP PIECE X 2

FRONT BOTTOM PIECE X 1

CUFF x 2

COLLAR x 2

1 Cut out the pattern pieces. Iron interfacing to cuffs, and collar pieces. Zigzag or overlock along all edges excerpt on collar and cuffs.

2 Place front and back with right sides facing and seam shoulders.

3 Fold tucks and sew at seam allowance. Place one long side of cuff with right sides facing at lower edge of each sleeve and sew down. Press seam toward cuff.

4 Pin sleeves into armholes with right sides facing. We think it is easiest to begin at the center of underarm and the two sides. Then pin the rest and ease in until even. Sew armhole seam.

5 Place collar pieces with right sides facing and seam along top curve. Press seam open; lay pieces with right sides facing and press.

6 Pin collar around neckline and join along one side. Press seam up toward collar. Do not sew rest of collar until the zipper has been inserted.

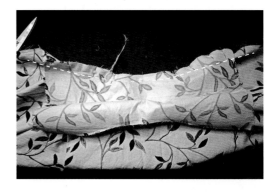

7 Open the zipper and pin it to one jacket front, all the way to the top of the collar. Sew in. Attach opposite side of zipper the same way.

8 Fold raw edge ⅜ in (1 cm) in toward collar and pin to inside. If you stitch from the right side, you'll have more control for a nicer look. Make sure you sew through all the layers.

9   Sew lower part of front with right sides facing. Press seam open.

10   Place one long side of cuff along lower edge of sleeve, with right sides facing. Seam. Press seam to cuff. Seam each side and sleeve, from lower edge out to cuff.

11   Fold cuff to wrong side to cover seam. Press and sew from front. Make sure you sew through all the layers.

12   Fold the lower edge of body to wrong side and sew down. You can fold a doubled hem if you prefer.

With a Hood

The hooded jacket is sewn as for the jacket with a collar except, of course, for the hood. Work though step 4 of the pattern with the collar and then skip to this page.

HOOD x 2

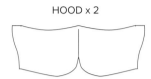

SEW THE HOOD:

1 Fold each of the hood pieces with right sides facing and seam down back of hood, from back neck to forehead.

2 Place hood pieces with right sides facing and seam front curve. Make sure you don't stitch in the place for the zipper.

3 With right sides facing, seam outermost part of hood to jacket.

4 Change to the zipper foot on your sewing machine. Sew in one side of zipper with right sides facing on outermost part of hood and down front of jacket. You can decide how much of the zipper tape you want showing and how close to the teeth to sew. When you reach the bottom stop and retaining box, lift the machine foot and pull the box underneath. Sew down the other side of the zipper the same way.

5 Fold in the innermost part of hood and sew hood along zipper and around back neck.

6 Continue to step 9 for jacket with collar.

Top with Puff Sleeves and Ruffled Neckband

Pattern Sheets: Ingrid Pullover

Fabric: We sewed the pullover from a shiny fabric.

Additional Materials: zipper, interfacing

Before You Begin: This top began with the basic pullover pattern, but we changed the sleeves to puff sleeves and edged the neckline with a ruffle instead of bias tape. To make the ruffles as fine as possible, the neck opening should be smaller. So, we added an invisible zipper to the back and cut the front neckline as for the back.

How to Cut Out Puff Sleeves: Find the center of the sleeve. Lay the sleeve template on the fabric and mark the center points at top and bottom + the width of lower edge. Shift the sleeve 4 in (10 cm) to the left and trim the shoulder curve all the way to the mark. Shift the sleeve 4 in (10 cm) to the right for the center point and trim away rest of shoulder curve. From the ends of the shoulder curve, cut a straight line down to the mark on lower edge of sleeve. If you want more puff, you can lengthen it by more than 4 in (10 cm). For very fine fabrics, you'll often need to lengthen even more for the same effect.

Pattern Pieces:

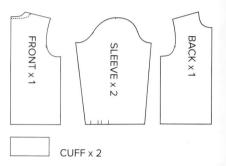

FRONT x 1
SLEEVE x 2
BACK x 1
CUFF x 2

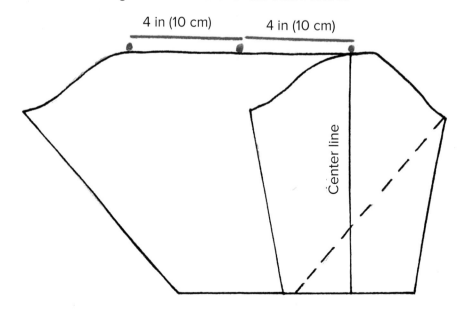

4 in (10 cm)   4 in (10 cm)

Center line

1 Cut out all the pullover pieces and configure the sleeves as puff sleeves as explained on previous page. Divide back pieces in two at center. Cut out all the pullover pieces. Cut back as two pieces by dividing at the center, adding ⅜ in (1 cm) seam allowance on each piece. Cut puff sleeves as described on page 44. The front neckline should match back neckline. Also cut a fabric strip for the ruffled neck. Determine the length of the strip by measuring the neckline and multiplying by 2.5. The height is 4 in (10 cm). Iron interfacing onto the strip, on the two cuffs, and along the sides of the back where the zipper will be inserted.

2 Place front and back pieces with right sides facing and seam shoulders.

3 Fold the neckband strip lengthwise, with right sides facing. Seam short ends. Trim corners to about ⅜ in (1 cm) from seamline; turn and press. Gather neckband to fit around neckline. Pin and then sew band around neck. Remove gathering threads, press seam down, and top stitch. See page 228 for more details on gathering.

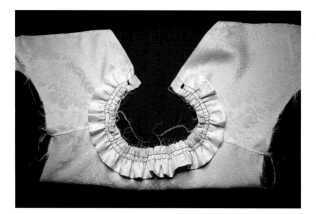

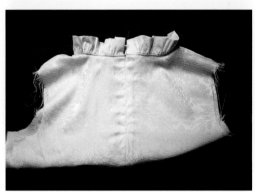

4 Insert an invisible zipper at center back of top. Mark top of zipper with two pins and place two pins 2 in (5 cm) from lower edge. Pin one side of zipper to top, all the way up to the base of ruffled neckband. Sew as close as possible to zipper teeth without sewing over teeth. Stop when you reach the pins indicating that 2 in (5 cm) remains of zipper. Make sure zipper is invisible by closing it. If you can still see the zipper, sew it again, more closely to the teeth. Pin the other side of the zipper and sew it in the same way. Stitch as close as possible along base of zipper.

5 Gather sleeves, with tightest gathers at center of each sleeve. Pin sleeves around armholes and then seam armholes.

6 Gather lower sleeve edge to fit cuff length. Sew down one long side of cuff to lower edge of sleeve, with right sides facing. Press seam toward cuff.

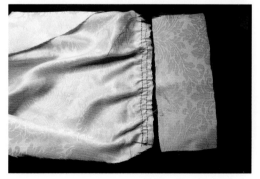

7 Sew side seams, from lower edge of top all the way to cuff.

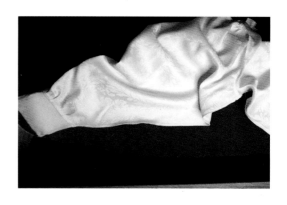

8 Fold cuff back to cover seam; press and sew from right side. Make sure seam goes through all layers.

9 Fold the lower edge of body to wrong side and sew down. You can fold a doubled hem if you prefer.

Top with Ruffles around Neckline

Pattern Sheets: Ingrid Pullover

Fabric: We recommend sewing this top with a firm but light fabric. We used a dotted cotton fabric that Ingrid VL inherited from a friend of her grandparents.

Additional Materials: ¼ in (0.5 cm) wide elastic band, sewing needle

Before You Begin: This top begins with the basic pullover pattern, but many changes are made as you work. Make sure you have enough fabric for the add-on ruffles.

Pattern Pieces:

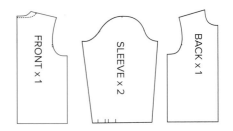

1 Cut out the back and front following the pattern.

6 in (15 cm)   6 in (15 cm)

8 in (20 cm)

Center line

2 Shorten the sleeves with the center line 8 in (20 cm) from the top down. Place the sleeve on the fabric and mark the center point above and below. Shift sleeve 6 in (15 cm) to the left and trim away shoulder curve to the marking. Shift sleeve 6 in (15 cm) to the right before the center point and trim away rest of shoulder curve. The lower edge of the sleeve stays the same.

3 Pin the front on your shoulders (we hope you have clothes on). Mark ⅜ in (1 cm) above where you want the base of the neckline. Cut a straight line from the top of the front and down to the marker on each side.

4 Measure the circumference around the neck. Cut a strip three times longer than the circumference and 6¾ in (17 cm) wide. If you don't have enough fabric, you can make the strip a bit shorter.

5 Zigzag or overlock all the pieces.

6 Place front on top of back with right sides facing and seam shoulders.

7 Stitch gathering threads along curve of shoulder. Pull in gathers until sleeve fits the curve between the front and back. With gathers pulled in along top of each sleeve, sew sleeves into armholes with right sides facing. You'll find more detailed information about gathering on page 229.

8 Seam sides from outer edge of sleeve to lower edge of top.

9 Sew gathering threads on the strip. Pull in gathers until strip fits around neckline. Make sure gathers are evenly distributed. Now you have a ruffle. Seam short sides of ruffle.

10 Sew right side of ruffle along neckline, on wrong side of top. Remove gathering threads and fold ruffle over to right side of top. Smooth ruffle with your fingers and top stitch through both layers ⅜ in (1 cm) from edge entirely around neckline.

11 Raise edge of ruffle and around armholes by folding ⅜ in (1 cm) to wrong side; sew down.

12 Measure length of elastic by holding it around your waist and deciding how tight you want it. Now make a casing. Fold and press the lowest edge 1⅜ in (3.5 cm) in toward wrong side. Sew around, but leave an opening. Stitch a line all the way around ⅜ in (1 cm) below previous casing stitch line. Attach a safety pin to one end of the elastic and draw it through the casing. Tie the ends. Sew hole closed.

13 With a sewing needle, stitch along shoulder seams using ⅜ in (1 cm) stitch lengths above and below the seam. Shift fabric so that shoulders draw together. Stitch a couple of times through all the ruffles and fasten off thread.

INGRID SHIRT

This shirt can be worn by men and women. It has a straight silhouette and can be shortened or lengthened as preferred. For a shirt with a more classic look, you should choose cotton fabric, such as, for example, a bedsheet. Cotton is the most common fabric for sewing shirts for a traditional look, but this shirt can also be sewn in a thinner fabric if you want a lighter look, or in a firmer, thicker fabric if you plan on wearing it as a shirt-jacket. We have sewn shirts in this book with a wool curtain, a thin flower-patterned curtain, and the base of a tent; that last one because we wanted to try to make a shirt with fabric that would be reminiscent of faux leather.

Wool Shirt-Jacket

Pattern Sheets: Ingrid Shirt

Fabric: a wool curtain

Additional Materials: snaps, interfacing

Before You Begin: If you want the shirt or the sleeves longer or shorter, make the adjustments before you cut out the fabric. Don't forget to mark the tucks and splits (also the little Y at the top).

Pattern Pieces:

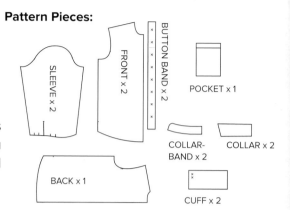

1 Cut out all the pieces. Iron the interfacing onto the collar pieces, front bands, and cuffs. Zigzag or overlock all edges except for the collar pieces, front bands, and cuffs.

2 Fold the tucks on the sleeves together as arrows on the pattern sheet shows, and sew them together to hold in place.

3 Place front on top of back with right sides facing and seam shoulders.

4 Fold lower edge of each sleeve at the split to wrong side and sew down.

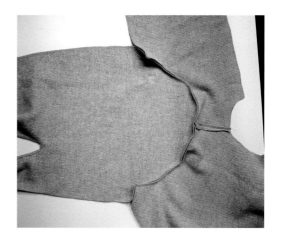

5 Pin sleeves into armholes with right sides facing. We think it is easiest to begin at the center and the two sides and then pin the rest evenly. Sew in sleeves.

6 Seam sides from outer edge of sleeve to the split.

7 Fold each cuff with right sides facing and seam short ends. Trim corners about 1/32 in (1 mm) from seam, turn and press.

8 Sew one side of cuff to right side of sleeve. Place cuff so that it points backward when it is buttoned.

9 Fold the other side of cuff ⅜ in (1 cm) in, press and pin to sleeve. If you stitch from the right side, you'll have more control for a nicer look. Make sure you sew through all layers. If the fabric is thick, as our wool curtain was, you can sew this side without folding it in. In that case, don't forget to zigzag or overlock along the raw edges.

10 Hem lower edge by folding it in and sewing it down. At the split, also fold the edge under and sew it down as shown in the photo.

11 Sew the front bands to the front pieces, with right sides facing. Press each seam toward band.

12 Fold front band lengthwise, with right sides facing. Seam at lower edges in line with hemmed edge.

13 Turn front band right side out. Fold in raw edges, pin and top stitch from right side. Make sure you stitch through all layers.

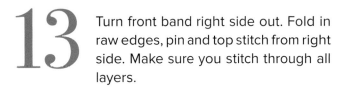

14 Place large collar pieces with right sides facing and seam all edges except for the shorter long side. Trim corners, turn and press.

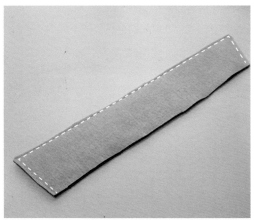

15 Place small collar pieces with right sides facing on each side of the large collar pieces. Seam through all layers. Cut two notches in seam allowance at each curve; turn and press.

16 Sew one edge of collar to outside of shirt, with right sides facing. Fold the other raw edge in toward collar and sew from outside of shirt. Make sure you stitch through all layers. If you are using a heavy fabric, you might want to sew the edge without folding it in. In that case, don't forget to zigzag or overlock along the raw edges.

17 Pocket: On one of the short sides, fold the edge in to wrong side by ⅜ in (1 cm). Stitch down. Fold the other sides in by ⅜ in (1 cm) and press. Pin pocket to shirt where shown on pattern sheet (or where you think it looks best), and stitch down.

18 Make buttonholes and sew buttons to button band and cuffs. To make a buttonhole, use the buttonhole foot (see sewing machine information for instructions).

19 Sew a tie belt in style you like. See how-to on page 232. For our wool shirt, we cut a strip 4¾ in (12 cm) wide and 61 in (155 cm) long.

Curtains

We made this shirt with a flower-patterned curtain.

Embroidered Cloth

We sewed this shirt from an inherited,
hand-embroidered cloth.

Ingrid Shirt with Puff Sleeves

The shirt with puff sleeves was sewn as for a regular shirt. The only difference is the sleeve shaping.

A Little about Pattern Placement

We sewed our puff sleeve shirt from an embroidered cloth. When sewing with embroidered fabric, it is a good idea to think about the placement of the embroidery on the garment. Embroidery on the chest is usually better than a clump of embroidery on your stomach. Symmetrical front and back pieces are pretty but not always possible. Many embroidered items are small, so the shirt often has to be fitted to the cloth you have. For example, we shortened our shirt to fit the pieces within the cloth we had. We recommend arranging all the pattern pieces on the cloth before you cut anything so you'll know how the puzzle will be solved.

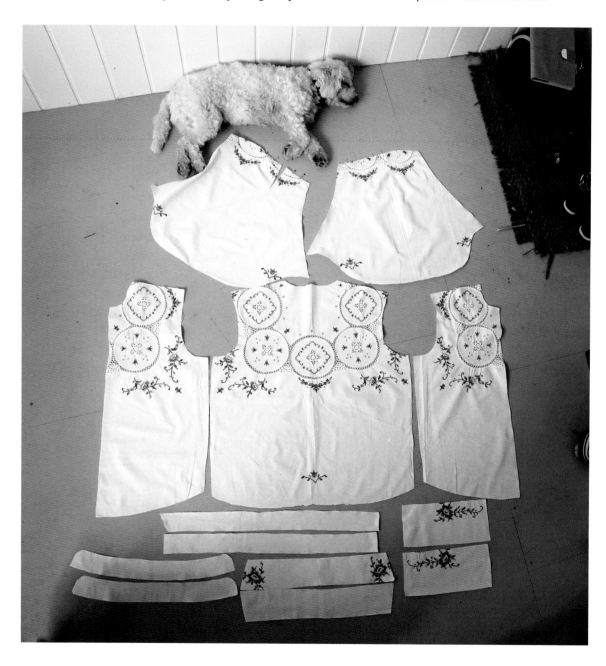

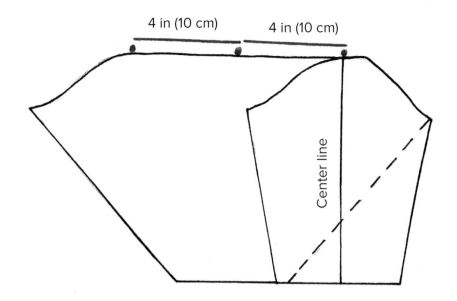

4 in (10 cm) 4 in (10 cm)

Center line

Cutting Puff Sleeves

Find the center of the sleeve (on pattern piece). Lay the sleeve on the fabric and mark the center points at top and bottom + the width of lower edge. Shift the sleeve 4 in (10 cm) to the left and trim the shoulder curve all the way to the marked point. Shift the sleeve 4 in (10 cm) to the right for the center point and trim away rest of shoulder curve. From the ends of the shoulder curve, cut a straight line down to the mark on lower edge of sleeve. If you want more puff, you can lengthen it by more than 4 in (10 cm). For very fine fabrics, you'll often need to lengthen the puff even more for the same effect.

Sewing Puff Sleeves

After seaming the front and back pieces of the shirt, attach sleeves. Gather along the shoulder cap. Pull gathering threads until sleeve fits curve between front and back. Arrange gathers at top of sleeve and sew in sleeves with right sides facing. See page 229 for more information about gathering.

DRESSES

The dresses in this chapter were sewn from many different fabrics. Use light, thin textiles for super summer dresses. You can also make fine everyday dresses in wool or cotton, or more elegant dresses in shiny fabrics and velvet. Dresses with ruffles and gathers need more fabric, so it might be a good idea to use long curtains, sheeting, or large cloths.

Dress with Balloon Sleeves

Pattern Sheets: Ingrid Pullover

Fabric: This dress can be sewn in many different types of fabric. Our dress was sewn with curtains from a thrift shop. One of our Instagram followers told us that these were the same curtains she had donated to that shop a few months before. So fun!

Additional Materials: If your fabric is thin, you can iron on interfacing as a facing, but we did not do that here.

Before You Begin: This dress is based on the pullover pattern, but lengthened. We lined the neckband on this dress to make it lie flat and smooth.

Pattern Pieces:

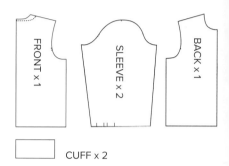

FRONT x 1   SLEEVE x 2   BACK x 1

CUFF x 2

1 Measure to determine how long you want the dress to be, from shoulders and down.

2 Cut out front and back as for regular pullover, adding as many inches (centimeters) as you need in length. My (Ingrid VL) front and back piece measures 30¾ in (78 cm) from the underarm down. The pullover pattern is roomy, so, for most figures, you can lengthen it straight down. If you need more room for your hips and backside, you can angle the pieces from the waist down.

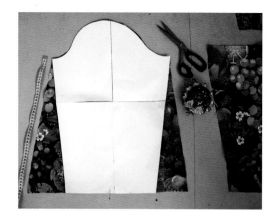

3 When you cut out the sleeves, add 4¾ in (12 cm) out on each side on lower edge. Cut a diagonal line up from the point to the curve. Make sure that this line is as long as on the pattern.

4 Use the neckline on front and back pieces to cut out the facing. Cut facing to exactly match neck outline. Make facing 2 in (5 cm) wide all the way across.

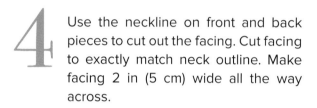

5 Cut waistband as a strip 8 in (20 cm) wide. Determine length of band by measuring your waist and adding enough length so you can tie a bow in the band. We cut ours 8 in (20 cm) by 77 in (196 cm). Join all the pieces you need (see page 232 for more details on tie belts).

6 Iron interfacing to facings and cuffs if the fabric is fine.

7 Sew on facings with right sides facing. Notch along seamlines. Fold seams to wrong side and press down.

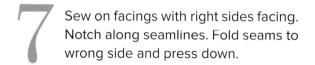

8 Place front and back with right sides facing, and seam shoulders and facing edges.

9 Gather lower edge of each sleeve. Pull gathers until same width as cuffs. Space gathers evenly (see page 229 for more details about gathering).

10 Sew one long side of each cuff to sleeve, with right sides facing. Remove gathering threads and press seam toward cuff.

11 Pin sleeve into armhole with right sides facing. We think it is easiest to begin with the center and two sides and then to pin the rest so spacing is even all around. Sew in each sleeve.

12

Sew side seam from lower edge of dress to top of cuffs. Press seams toward cuff.

13

Fold cuff to inside of sleeve. Fold in raw edges ⅜ in (1 cm), press and sew on cuffs. If you stitch from the right side, you'll have more control for a nicer look. Make sure you stitch through all layers.

14

Hem lower edge by folding it to wrong side and sewing it own. Fold a doubled hem if you like.

15

With right sides facing, seam strip for tie belt. Turn right side out and press (see page 232 for more details).

Elegant Ruffled Dress

Pattern Sheets: Ingrid Pullover

Fabric: This dress can be sewn in many different types of fabric. If you use a finer fabric, the gathers will stand out less than if you use a heavier fabric. We used a medium-weight creamy white curtain.

Additional Materials: interfacing, bias tape for neckline

Before You Begin: This dress combines the pullover pattern with two layers of ruffles sewn one under the other. Begin with your own measurements to determine the length and width.

Pattern Pieces:

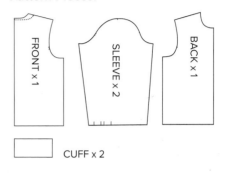

1 Measure your body from the neck down to the length you want the dress to be. Ours ended at about the middle of the thigh. Divide the measurement into three equal parts. The first part is for the length of the top, from the neck down; the other two parts are for the ruffle layers.

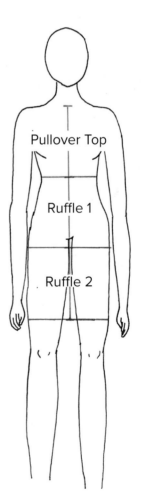

2 Cut out all the pattern pieces for the pullover top. Shorten the front and back following your own measurements as explained in step 1. Cut out a bias tape (see page 230 for details).

3 Here's how to calculate the width of the ruffle layers: measure the width of the front of the lower edge of pullover top and multiply by 5—this is the width of ruffle 1. Multiply the width of ruffle 1 by 2.5 for ruffle 2. Now both ruffles are 2.5 times as long as the circumference of the top. This requires a large piece of fabric, and, if you don't have enough or want smaller ruffles, you can multiply by a smaller number.

Circumference of lower edge of pullover top × 2.5
Ruffle 1

Ruffle 1 × 2.5
Ruffle 2

4 Zigzag or overlock all edges except for the cuffs and around the neck. Place front and back with right sides facing and seam shoulders.

5 Sew bias tape around neckline. See page 230 for more details.

6 Pin sleeves into armholes with right sides facing. We think it is easiest to begin at the center and two sides and then pin the rest so the sleeves fit in evenly. Sew in sleeves.

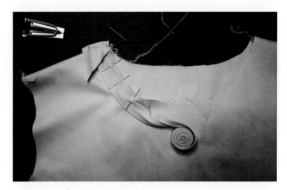

7 Gather lower edges of sleeves and pull gathering threads until sleeve edge matches cuff width. Divide gathers evenly. See page 229 for more information about gathering. Place each cuff on sleeve with right sides facing and stitch between the two gathering threads. Remove gathering threads and press seam toward cuff.

8 Seam each side from lower edge of bodice to cuff. Fold seams toward cuffs.

9 Fold back each cuff to cover seamline, press and sew down from right side.

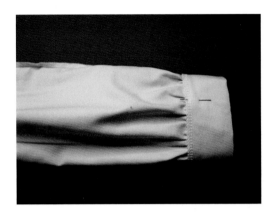

10 If you cut the ruffle panels from several pieces of fabric, seam them and join each band into a ring.

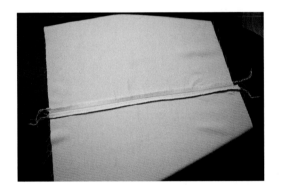

11 Fold in hem on lower ruffle panel to wrong side and sew down. Make a doubled hem if you prefer.

12 Gather lower ruffle panel so circumference matches that of upper panel. See page 229 for more information about gathering.

13 Pin lower ruffle to upper one. Space gathers as evenly as possible and make sure that the fabric doesn't fold and double. There is a lot of fabric to control. Stitch centered between the two gathering lines. Remove gathering threads and press panels.

14 Gather top ruffle panel to match lower edge of bodice. Pin and then sew panel to bodice. Remove gathering threads and press.

Shirtdress

Pattern Sheets: Ingrid Shirt

Fabric: This dress was sewn from a pretty fabric inherited from a friend of Ingrid VL's grandparents. For this dress, we recommend a light, soft fabric. Because the dress requires a fair amount of fabric, a comforter cover or similar large piece of fabric will work best.

Additional Materials: zipper, interfacing

Before You Begin: The shirtdress is a lengthened version of the shirt pattern in the book, with an added tie belt. Don't forget to mark the tucks and side splits (also the little Y at the top). The side splits are 4¾ in (12 cm) long.

Pattern Pieces:

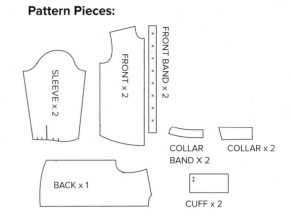

SLEEVE x 2
FRONT x 2
FRONT BAND x 2
COLLAR BAND X 2
COLLAR x 2
BACK x 1
CUFF x 2

---

1 You'll need your measuring tape to begin. Measure how long you want the dress to be from your shoulders down. Cut out the pattern pieces for the front and back and cut them across the center. Lay the pieces on the fabric, as far from each other as you need to lengthen them. As an example, I lengthened (Ingrid VL) by 13½ in (34 cm) (although I am actually only 5 feet, 2½ in (159 cm) tall. The shirt pattern is roomy, so lengthening it straight down works for most figures. If you need extra room for your hips and backside, you can angle the sides out from the waist down.

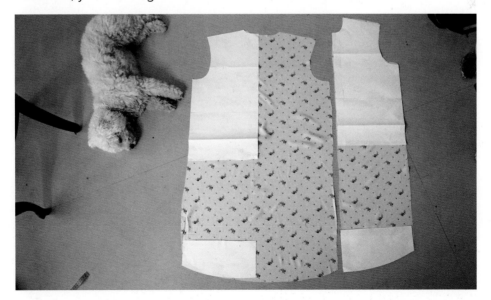

2 To calculate the length of the front bands, measure the front piece you cut out, from center front at the neck and down.

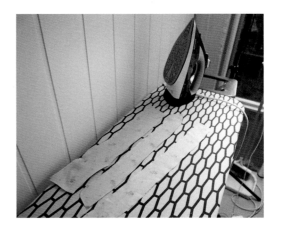

3 Iron interfacing onto the collar pieces, front bands and cuffs. Zigzag or overlock all the edges except those on the collar pieces, front bands and cuffs.

4 Fold up lower sleeve edges at split to wrong side and sew down. Fold tucks in same direction as arrows show in pattern, and stitch at seamline to hold them in place.

5 Place front and back with right sides facing and seam shoulders.

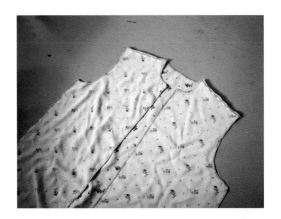

6 Pin sleeves into armholes with right sides facing. We think it is easiest to begin at the center and two sides and then pin the rest so the sleeves fit in evenly. Sew in sleeves.

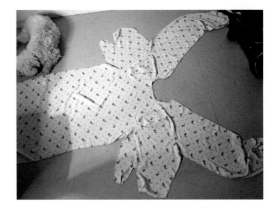

7 Seam each side from outer edge of sleeves to split, which should be 4¾ in (12 cm) long. Fold seams toward cuffs.

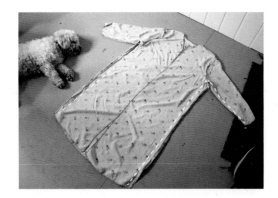

8 Fold cuffs with right sides facing and seam short ends. Trim corners, turn and press.

9 Sew one end of cuff to right side of sleeve so cuff points back where it will be buttoned.

10 Fold in other side by ⅜ in (1 cm), press, and pin to sleeve. If you stitch from the right side, you'll have more control for a nicer look. Make sure you stitch through all layers.

11 Hem lower edge of dress by folding it in and sewing down. Also fold in the edges of splits and sew down.

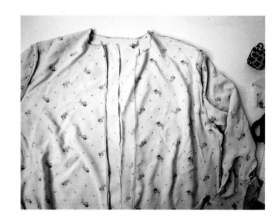

12 Sew front bands to front with right sides facing. Press seam toward band.

13 Fold front bands lengthwise with right sides facing and seam along lower edge, aligned with hemmed edge.

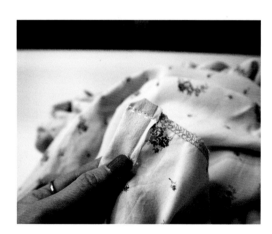

14 Turn front bands back. Fold in raw edges, pin and sew, stitching from right side. Make sure you stitch through all layers.

15 Place large collar pieces with right sides facing and sew along all edges except the shorter long side. Trim corners about 1/32 in (1 mm) from seam, turn and press. Place small collar pieces with right sides facing on each side of larger collar pieces. Seam through all layers. Cut two notches to seam line on each curve; turn and press.

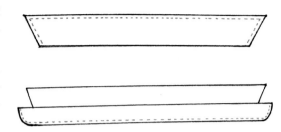

16 Sew one edge of collar to outside of dress, with right sides facing. Fold the other raw edge into collar and sew down from outside.

17 Make buttonholes and sew on buttons to front bands and cuffs. To make buttonholes, use the buttonhole foot on your sewing machine (see your sewing machine instructions). Space buttonholes 4 in (10 cm) apart.

18 Choose your style of tie belt and sew one. See page 232 for details. We cut a strip 6 in (15 cm) wide and 63 in (160 cm) long.

Dress with Shoulder Ruffles

Fabric: We sewed our dresses with viscose fabric and an embroidered cloth. This dress works with most fabrics that are light and comfortable to wear. If you use a stiffer fabric, the shoulder ruffles will stand out more than those on our dresses.

Before You Begin: This dress begins with the top you've seen here before. Use a top in a sturdy fabric that will fit a bit loosely on you. If you want a tight-fitting top, add ¾–1¼ in (2–3 cm) seam allowance so the dress won't be too tight.

1 Lay the top on the fabric. Decide how long you want the dress to be by measuring or laying on the fabric. Cut around the top, adding ⅜ in (1 cm) around the edges. When you've cut out one half, fold it over and cut out the rest so the piece will be symmetrical.

2 Use the first piece to cut out an identical piece. Cut the neck opening larger on the piece that will be the front. To ensure that the neck will be large enough, pin the front fabric to your shoulders and pull the dress on over your head.

3 Zigzag or overlock all edges.

4 Place back and front together with right sides facing and seam top at shoulders and on side, from underarm to lower edge of dress.

5 Fold in edge of neck and lower edge of dress about ⅜ in (1 cm) to wrong side and sew down. You can also fold a double hem if you want.

6 Now it's time to make the ruffles. Cut out two circles with the measurements shown here. Make a paper template with an opening first. Zigzag or overlock all the edges.

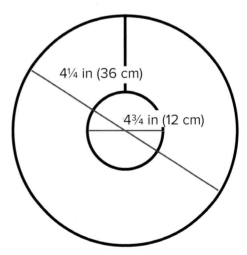

4¼ in (36 cm)

4¾ in (12 cm)

7 Gather along the inside edge of each ruffle (see page 229 for more details on gathering). Pull gathers until inside edge is about 9¾ in (25 cm) or place ruffle at your shoulder and decide how much ruffling you want.

8 With right sides facing, sew inside edge of ruffle to shoulder. The actual opening in the ring should also be included. Fold edge of armhole to wrong side and sew down.

9 Sew a tie belt if you want (see page 232 for details).

Dress with Ruffled Hem

Fabric: We made ours with a comforter cover. We recommend fabric from clothes, sheeting, thin curtains, or stretchy fabric. Really, there is nothing to prevent you from using what you like for this dress. Since the dress has ruffles on both hem and sleeves, you'll need more fabric than for a regular dress.

Additional Materials: a slightly oversized T-shirt

Before You Begin: This dress was sewn without a pattern, instead using a slightly oversized T-shirt as the template. You can decide on the total length and circumference of the dress—ours is rather oversized.

1   Cut out the front and back. These are exactly the same. Before cutting them out, lay a large T-shirt on the fabric and cut around it. Don't forget that T-shirts are often stretchy while cloth or sheeting is not, so you need to add a little extra fabric all over and cut the neckline large enough to fit over your head.

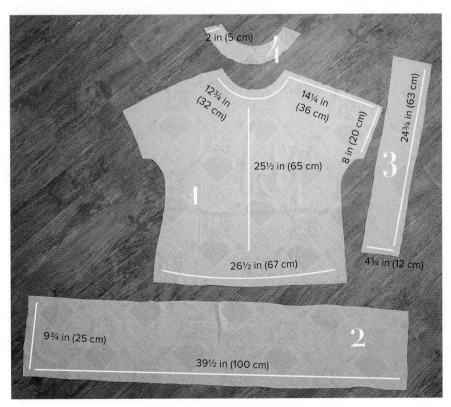

2 Zigzag or overlock all the edges. Iron interfacing onto the two facings.

3 Place back and front together with right sides facing and seam shoulders; press. Seam sides, from underarm to lower edge of dress.

4 Lay the two facing pieces over each other with right sides facing and sew them together along the short sides.

5 With right sides facing, lay facing around neckline. Sew along upper edge.

6 Join all the pieces for the lower ruffle. Ours had four sections, and we joined them into a large circle.

7 Hem lower edge by pressing a seam ⅝ in (1.5 cm) under and sew a seam to hold it in place.

8 Gather ruffle all around top edge and pull in gathers until it fits lower edge of dress. See page 229 for more details on gathering.

9 Pin and then sew ruffle to lower edge of dress.

10 Make ruffles for sleeves as for lower edge of dress.

This dress
begins with a
shirt pattern
and features a
long skirt with
two ruffled
panels.

Using the shirt pattern as a
starting point, this dress adds
a long skirt and two ruffles.

Maxi Dress

Pattern Sheets: Ingrid Shirt

Fabric: Our maxi dress was sewn from cotton bed sheeting. Soft, light, and fine fabrics are best for this dress, but it would certainly be impressive in a heavier fabric. The gathered tiers require a lot of fabric, so you might consider combining several fabrics.

Additional Materials: buttons, interfacing, ¼ in (0.5 cm) wide elastic

Before You Begin: Measure the length from neck to your waist, adjusting the length on front and back of the shirt pattern so the length is ⅜ in (1 cm) longer than your measurements.

Pattern Pieces:

SLEEVE x 2 · FRONT x 2 · KNAPPESTOLPE x 2 · COLLAR BAND X 2 · BACK x 1 · CUFF x 2

1 Cut out all the pieces you need. Iron interfacing onto the collar pieces, front bands, and cuffs.

2 Cut out the skirt and the two gathered panels as follows: Measure yourself from the waist to desired hem of skirt. Divide this measurement into three large pieces. The length of the skirt is the same length as two panels. I (Ingrid B) then measured from waist to hem, 39 in (99 cm). Divided by 3 = 13 in (33 cm). That makes the skirt 26 in (66 cm) long. The panels are each 13 in (33 cm) long. The length of the skirt is the same as the width of the shirt. To calculate the length of the two gathered panels, measure the width of the skirt and multiply by 2.5.

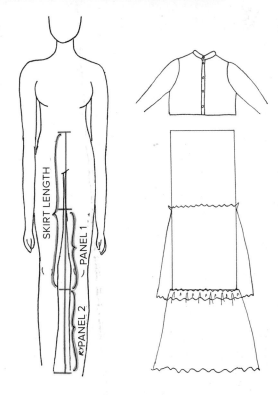

3 Zigzag or overlock all edges except on the collar pieces, cuffs, and front bands. Fold sleeve tucks as indicated by the arrows on the pattern sheet and stitch at seamline. On lower edge of sleeve, fold edges of split to wrong side and sew down.

4 Place front and back with right sides facing and seam shoulders.

5 Pin and then sew sleeves into armholes.

6 Sew front bands to front with right sides facing. Press seam toward band. Fold in raw edges, pin and then sew from right side. Make sure you stitch through all layers.

7 Place collar pieces with right sides facing and sew together except along lower edge (outer curve). Clip two notches in each of the curves; turn and press.

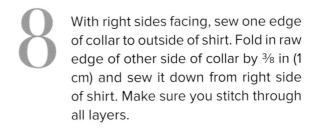

8 With right sides facing, sew one edge of collar to outside of shirt. Fold in raw edge of other side of collar by ⅜ in (1 cm) and sew it down from right side of shirt. Make sure you stitch through all layers.

9 Seam sides from lower edge of shirt and down to split.

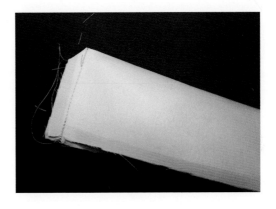

10 Fold cuff with right sides facing and seam short sides. Trim corners, turn, and press.

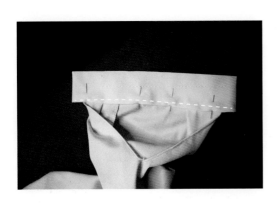

11 Sew one long side of cuff to right side of sleeve so cuff is even all around. Press seam toward cuff. Fold the other raw edge in ⅜ in (1 cm), press, and pin to sleeve. If you stitch from the right side, you'll have more control for a nicer look. Make sure you stitch through all layers.

12 Place front bands over each other and seam along lower edge to hold them in place while you attach them to the skirt.

13 With right sides facing, seam skirt into a cylinder. Press the seam open and turn. Place skirt and shirt with right sides facing. To make a casing for the waist elastic, place the shirt ¾ in (2 cm) below skirt. Sew the pieces together and press seam open. The longer band of the seam, which is now ironed down toward the skirt, will be the casing.

14 Making sure that the band is wide enough for the elastic, seam all around the casing band, leaving a small opening so you can insert the elastic.

15 Measure elastic to fit your waist. Attach a safety pin to end of elastic and draw elastic through casing. Knot ends of elastic. Stitch casing opening closed.

16 Sew the top gathered panel first. With right sides facing, sew the panel pieces together into a ring. Press seams open. Fold up lower edge ⅜ in (1 cm) to wrong side and sew down. Gather upper edge and pull in until it fits circumference of skirt. See more about gathering on page 229.

17 Measure the length from elastic at waist down to place where gathered panel will be attached. Mark where skirt will be attached with chalk, pins or a marker pen.

18 Pin gathered panel to outside of skirt with wrong side facing right side following markings. Sew on between the two gathering threads. Remove gathering threads and press.

19 Sew lower panel into a ring as for first panel and pin to lower edge of skirt. Sew on between the two gathering threads. Remove gathering threads and press.

20 Make buttonholes and sew buttons on front band and cuffs. To make buttonholes, use buttonhole foot of your machine and see machine instructions.

Festive Dress (Bunad)

Sewing festive traditional garments like this is a subject all its own. A traditional Norwegian folk costume (*bunad*) requires a great deal of work, with hand stitching and embroidery, and knowledge of tradition. We are certainly not experts on tradition but, at the same time, want to show how it's possible to make your own fantastic festive dress of recycled textiles without it being too difficult. This festive dress has a lot of room for variation. It can be enhanced with ribbons, embroidery, and beads or kept completely simple. We would love to see your variations!

Fabric: For the festive dress, you'll need heavy, strong fabric, such as wool and brocade. The dress gives you the opportunity to experiment with all sorts of fabric combinations. We used curtains. The skirt was sewn with an embroidered cloth and sheer curtain.

Additional Materials: 16 in (40 cm) invisible zipper, interfacing, decorative ribbon ¾–1¼ in (2–3 cm wide)

Before You Begin: The festive dress is constructed with a skirt sewn together with a vest-like top, or a bodice—*liv* in bunad terminology. You don't need pattern sheets. We'll help you construct the outfit from your own measurements. The shirt for the dress is made following the pattern for the shirt with puff sleeves.

BEGIN WITH THE SKIRT

1 Take your measurements from your breast down to your ankle. The skirt has one piece, this length × 3⅓ yd (3 m). You can combine several pieces to have enough fabric.

2 Zigzag or overlock all the edges.

3 Sew four gathering lines each ⅜ in (1 cm) apart at top of skirt. The gathering threads won't be removed later on, so use an extra-strong thread the same color as the fabric (see page 229 for more details on gathering).

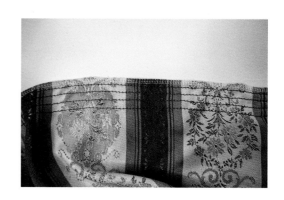

4 Draw in gathering threads until skirt is approximately same circumference as just below your breasts. Divide gathers evenly. Set skirt aside.

CONSTRUCTING THE TOP

5 Measure circumference around largest area of bust, wearing a bra (if you usually wear one) and thin shirt or top. Measure vertically over your breasts, from 2 in (5 cm) below the breasts to the point where you want the top to end, approximately right over the breast. Add ⅜ in (1 cm) seam allowance and cut out a rectangle with these measurements. For example, my measurements here are 9¾ × 36 in (25 × 91 cm).

6 Pin top at height you want it, with the opening at the front. Measure for the length of the straps. The straps go straight up the front but are diagonal on the back to meet at the center—they do not cross. Add 2 in (5 cm) to make sure you cut the straps long enough—you can trim off any extra later. Cut two bands to your length × 3½ in (9 cm). Mine are 20½ × 3½ in (52 × 9 cm).

7 Iron interfacing to whole top and straps and zigzag or overlock all edges. We used a heavy interfacing so the top would be stiff enough.

8 Fold in the edges of the straps to the wrong side so the straps will be 2½ in (6.5 cm) wide. Press and sew down.

9 Pin the straps to the top with right sides facing. They should meet at center back. Try the top on to make sure the straps sit correctly. Sew them on.

10 Turn in edges at center front 1 in (2.5 cm) and sew down. This stitching will be visible, so be extra careful.

11 Try on top and use pins to mark placement of skirt around top. The skirt might hang longer at the front than at the back of the top. Place the decorative ribbons with right sides facing along the markings and sew them along lower edge. Let ½–2 in (4–5 cm) of ribbon hang out on each end.

JOIN TOP AND SKIRT

12 Measure decorative ribbon, from edge of front top to edge of other side. Adjust the gathers on the skirt so they are an even width + ¾ in (2 cm). Sew all the gathering threads to the wrong side of the fabric and fasten them off well.

13 Place skirt on top, with wrong side facing right side, directly below decorative ribbon. Sew skirt to top along seam allowance of skirt, directly above gathers. Leave ⅜ in (1 cm) of skirt sticking out on each side of front.

14

Now it's time to insert the zipper into the skirt front. Place zipper right sides facing along one edge and sew in. Stitch as close to the zipper teeth as possible without sewing over them. Sew down the other side of the zipper the same way. (In the photo, you'll see that we used a visible zipper, but we recommend that it still be hidden.)

15

Seam the skirt below the zipper. By hand, sew the decorative ribbon on the inside and stitch a little by hand on back if necessary.

16

Fold the decorative ribbon over the seam of the skirt and sew down by hand.

RIBBON ON LOWER EDGE OF SKIRT IF YOU LIKE

17 Cut a strip 3⅓ yd × 4 in (3 m × 10 cm) (you can splice pieces if need be). Zigzag or overlock along one edge and sew the strip into a ring. Pin the strip to the skirt with right sides facing, 3¼ in (8 cm) from the lower edge. Sew along one edge of the ribbon so you can fold the ribbon down and over on the right side. Fold the ribbon around the lower edge of the skirt and sew down.

RIBBON AROUND WAIST

18 Cut ribbon or make a tie band, following details on page 232. The ribbon should be 1¼ in (3 cm) wide and as long as you need to tie around your waist at the top of the skirt and extending to hem of dress. I (Ingrid VL) made a tie band with the same fabric as the skirt and sewed the decorative ribbon onto it, so it would hold on well.

Ball Gown

This pattern shows how you can transform any regular dress into a formal gown without cutting or changing the original. Ball gowns are often worn only once, and many people spend a significant amount of money for them. Now you can upcycle an existing dress into a rather elegant gown.

Fabric: Tulle, silk lining, and a dress you like the top of

Additional Materials: interfacing, snaps

Before You Begin: This ball gown is made by making a skirt you can wear over another dress. The skirt consists of underskirt with tulle over it and a waistband. Note these measurements: hips, waist, from waist down to desired length of skirt. We made a full-length ball gown.

1 Cut out waistband, 4¾ in (12 cm) wide and length for your waist measurement + 2¾ in (7 cm). The length includes ⅜ in (1 cm) seam allowance. The width of the underskirt is your hip measurement × 1.5, with the length from your waist down to desired length of skirt. Cut 6.56 yd (6 m) of tulle with length as for skirt + ¾ in (2 cm) seam allowance.

2 Sew the underskirt. Fold skirt with right sides facing and sew side seam. At the same time, make a split from lower edge of skirt to middle of thigh, and a 6 in (15 cm) split at top.

3 Gather the top edge and draw in to fit your waist (see page 229 for more details on gathering).

4 Iron on interfacing to waistband. Fold band, with right sides facing and seam each end. Trim corners about 1/32 in (1 mm) from seam, turn and press.

5 Sew tulle into a ring with a 6 in (15 cm) split at top.

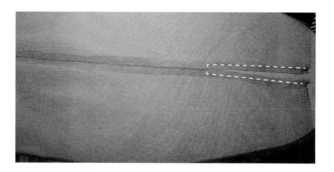

6 Gather the tulle and draw in to fit your waist (see page 229 for more details on gathering).

7 Pin and then sew tulle to one section of waistband with right sides facing. Begin 1 in (2.5 cm) from edge of band on each short end. Remove gathering threads.

8 Pin and then sew underskirt over tulle; remove gathering threads and press seam up.

9 Fold raw edges to waistband ⅜ in (1 cm) in, press and pin to inside of skirt. If you stitch from the right side, you'll have more control for a nicer look. Make sure you stitch through all layers.

10 Try on skirt over bodice and use pins to mark where you want to attach the snaps. Sew on snaps by hand.

When the Ingrid Jacket launched it was so well received that we went on an Ingrid Jacket tour and taught hundreds of beginners. It was so cool to see how one pattern led to so many completely different jackets. The Ingrid Jacket was designed so you can sew on a hood or collar, straight or billowy sleeves, and make it short or long. The perfect touch is matching the garment to the recycled fabric you have on hand.

INGRID JACKET

The Ingrid Jacket can be made from many different textiles. We'll show you how to make a blanket jacket, a rain jacket, and a puffy jacket from the Ingrid Jacket basic pattern.

The jacket is slightly oversized, so if you fall between two sizes, either will likely work. One might be a little more oversized than the other. The pattern sheets have lines for short and long versions, but we tend to adapt the length regardless of the markings. You can also do that, but take into consideration the information below. To cut to the length you want, hold the pattern front on your body and look in the mirror. Fold the pattern sheet to the length you want.

For inspiration, check us out on Instagram. And post pictures of your jacket when it's finished!

Blanket Jacket

Pattern Sheet: Ingrid Jacket

Fabric: We used a wool blanket from a flea market for our jacket. The jacket can be sewn with wool fabric, a lap rug, or furniture fabrics, but with thinner and fine textiles, this can be a summer jacket. You can also combine several textiles to make unique color combinations. If you do combine several fabrics, we recommend that they all be the same thickness.

Additional Materials: large press stud buttons

Before You Begin: Our jacket has fringe at the lower edge, so the lower edge is trimmed completely straight across. If you make the jacket without fringe, check the pattern for the rain jacket to see how you can sew the lower edge.

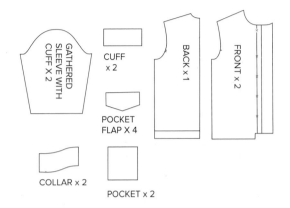

1 Cut out all the pieces. Zigzag or overlock all the edges except on the collar and pocket flaps. If you are making a short jacket, don't forget to see how you finish the lower edge.

2 Place the front and back with right sides facing, and seam shoulders.

3 Pin sleeves into armholes with right sides facing. We think it is easiest to begin at the center and the two sides and then pin the rest so the sleeves will be attached evenly. Sew in sleeves.

4 For full sleeves: Gather the sleeve so it is the same circumference as the cuff. Place cuff on sleeve with right sides facing, sew pieces together and press seam toward cuff. (See page 229 for more details on gathering.)

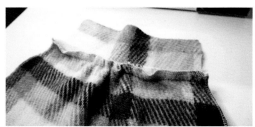

5 Seam sides from wrist to lower edge of jacket. Make sure that the seams meet at the underarms.

6 For full sleeves: Fold cuff in, making sure it lies over the seam on the inside. Stitch cuff in place from the right side. If you stitch in the space between the sleeve and cuff, the seam will be invisible. The cuff can also be sewn on by hand.

7 For straight sleeves: fold sleeve edge in and sew down.

8 Fold front band 3 in (7.5 cm) to wrong side of fabric and sew down.

9 Place collar pieces with right sides facing. Seam along all sides except lower edge (it curves in). Trim corners, turn and press. Place collar with right sides facing on jacket and sew outer section of collar. On inside of jacket, fold the edge on second collar piece ⅜ in (1 cm) in and sew it so all the seam along the collar is hidden. If you are sewing with heavy fabric, as for example, a lap rug, we recommend you sew this seam by hand.

10 Place pocket flaps with right sides facing. Pin and then sew them along all edges except for the top. Trim corners, turn and press. Top stitch ¼ in (0.5 cm) from edge around all sides except the top.

11 Pockets: Fold top edge ¾ in (2 cm) down to wrong side and top stitch to hold in place. Press the other three sides ⅝ in (1.5 cm) in. Pin and sew pockets where you want them.

12 Place pocket flaps ¾ in (2 cm) above pocket, with tip pointing up. Sew flap on lower edge. Fold it over. Press and top stitch to hold flap down and hide raw edges.

13 Sew on buttons of your choice. We used large press studs for our jackets.

Raincoat

Pattern Sheet: Ingrid Jacket

Fabric: We used waxed cotton cloth for this jacket, but any waterproof or water-resistant fabrics will work. Very thin fabrics will give the jacket a different look.

Additional Materials: press stud buttons, iron-on seam binding

Before You Begin: To make this jacket waterproof, cover all the inside seams with seam binding. Test to make sure the fabric can be ironed. If not, you can tape all the seams and then carefully iron only the taped seams.

Pattern Pieces:

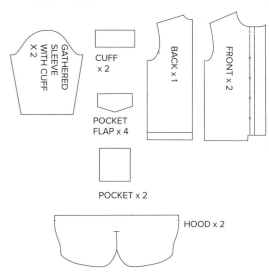

GATHERED SLEEVE WITH CUFF x 2

CUFF x 2

POCKET FLAP x 4

POCKET x 2

BACK x 1

FRONT x 2

HOOD x 2

This jacket is sewn as for the blanket jacket (see page 117) except for the hood, and there is no fringe at lower edge. Also, the seams are covered with iron-on seam binding to ensure that the jacket is waterproof. Follow the instructions on the seam binding package so you'll know the correct temperature to use for fusing the tape.

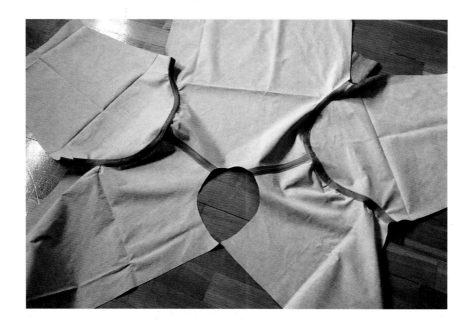

LOWER PART OF JACKET:

1 Fold front band 3 in (7.5 cm) to right side of fabric.

2 Stitch lower edge.

3 Trim corner to seam and fold band back.

4 Press fold all the way up and sew down.

5 Finish jacket lower edge by folding edge to wrong side so it aligns with front band. Sew down.

HOOD:

1 Place hood pieces with right sides facing and sew both back hood seams.

2 Press and turn.

3 Place hood and jacket with right sides facing, pin and sew back neck seam. Do not stitch though both layers of the hood—only the outermost layer.

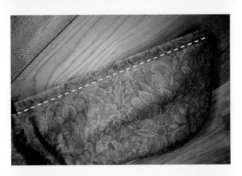

4 Fold hood over neck seam. Fold seam in, pin and sew down. This seam can also be sewn by hand because the fabric is right for that.

5 Press folded edge around face and top stitch.

Puffy Jacket

Pattern Sheet: Ingrid Jacket

Fabric: You'll need an old comforter/quilt for this pattern, outer fabric, and lining fabric. We used a down comforter that Ingrid VL got from a neighbor, as well as fabric she inherited from an old woman who moved to a nursing home and couldn't take along her fabric collection. Our jacket used the same fabric for the outside shell and lining. You might want to go up a size larger than usual, because filled jackets run small.

Additional Materials: press stud buttons, zipper (same length as jacket from collar down; ours is 27½ in [70 cm]).

Before You Begin: This is one of the most difficult and time-consuming patterns in the book. Make a regular variation of the Ingrid Jacket first if you are a beginner. To make a puffy Ingrid Jacket, you first sew a jacket with the outer fabric, one with the lining, and then one with the comforter before you join all three jackets. Since the Ingrid Jacket is oversized, you can cut the jacket for the size you normally wear or a size larger. Use ⅜ in (1 cm) seam allowances.

Pattern pieces, outer jacket, lining + quilting:

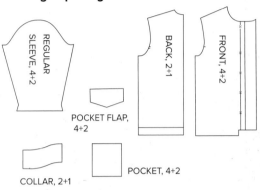

REGULAR SLEEVE, 4+2

BACK, 2+1

FRONT, 4+2

POCKET FLAP, 4+2

COLLAR, 2+1

POCKET, 4+2

1 Cut two sets of Ingrid Jacket pieces: one in the outer fabric and one in the lining fabric. Lengthen collar by 2 in (5 cm) at center back. The length of the jacket can be adjusted to fit the zipper. The zipper goes all the way up to top of collar.

2 Place the pattern pieces on the comforter and trace them with a good visible marker. Stitch along the lines right through the comforter. Push down/filling into the pieces and make sure all the pieces are about the same thickness.

3 Cut around all the pieces about ¼ in (0.5 cm) outside the seam (have your vacuum cleaner ready—there will be a lot of filling/down). Spread the comforter seams open so the down/filling can move freely in the piece.

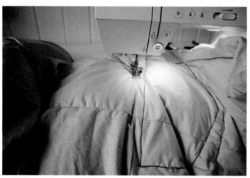

SEW THE OUTER, LINING, AND DOWN JACKETS SEPARATELY:

4 Place front and back with right sides facing and seam shoulders. Pin sleeves into armholes with right sides facing. We think it is easiest to begin at the center and the two sides and then pin the rest so the sleeves will be attached evenly. Sew in sleeves.

5 Seam sleeves and sides from wrist to lower edge of jacket. Make sure that the seams meet at the underarms.

6 Sew the comforter jacket the same way, but the pieces do not need to be seamed on the wrong side. You can lay the pieces next to each other, with right side facing wrong side. The sleeves should be sewn in as usual, which you'll get to later.

HOW TO SEW THE POCKETS AND COLLAR TO COMFORTER JACKET:

7 POCKET FLAPS: Place each pair of pocket flaps together with right sides facing and sew along all edges except lower edge. Trim corners 1/16 in (2 mm) from seam. Turn and push down pieces inside.

POCKET: Place pocket pieces together with right sides facing and sew along all edges except top edge. Trim corners 1/16 in (2 mm) from seam. Turn and push down pieces inside. On pocket itself, fold the top edge in and stitch top edge.

8 Place collar pieces with right sides facing and stitch along top edge (which curves up).

NOW JOIN THE THREE JACKETS:

9 Place outer and lining jackets with right sides facing and seam back neck and along lower edges. Turn and push comforter jacket inside.

10

Sew one collar piece to outer side of jacket with right sides facing. Trim about an inch (a couple of centimeters) along fronts of outer and lining jackets so they align with collar (if necessary; on the original Ingrid Jacket, this forms a part of the front bands).

11

Change to the zipper foot on your sewing machine. Place zipper with right sides facing on outer jacket and stitch one side down. Do the same with the other side. Fold edge of lining jacket in, pin it along zipper, and stitch through all layers. You will have more control if you stitch from the right side.

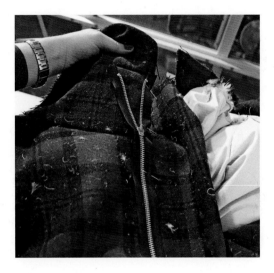

12

Push down piece into collar, fold edge of collar in, and sew collar to inside of jacket by hand.

13

Fold lower edges of sleeves of outer and lining jackets toward each other and seam by hand.

MAKE PUFFY "BUBBLES":

14

Many down/filled jackets are divided into equal blocks. Measure and stitch through all three layers to make "bubbles" in your jacket. Before you sew, it's a good idea to use pins or chalk to mark the stitching lines. For our jacket, we have three bubbles each on the front and back and none on the sleeves. You can decide how many bubbles you want. We also stitched blocks of bubbles on the pockets.

SEW ON THE POCKETS:

15

Pin and stitch on the pockets where you want them. Place pocket flaps ¾ in (2 cm) above the pocket, with the tip pointing upward. Sew flap along lower edge and then fold it over. Top stitch to hold flap down and hide the raw edges.

JUMPSUIT

A jumpsuit is a great garment for everyday dressing up or for getting cozy in comfy clothes. In this chapter, you'll learn how to transform a dress into a jumpsuit and how to use the patterns for the pullover to make a jumpsuit from scratch. We also include a pattern for a two-piece jogging outfit.

Jumpsuit

Pattern Sheet: Ingrid Pullover and Ingrid Pants

Fabric: We made our jumpsuit with a heavy, blue cotton curtain. We recommend slightly heavier fabrics that will be comfortable to wear and that breathe so the garment won't be too tight.

Additional Materials: two 5 in (12 cm) zippers, one 25 in (65 cm) zipper, interfacing elastic thread

Before You Begin: To make this jumpsuit, we used the pattern for straight pants (without a waistband) and, for the top, sporty pullover with a collar (omitting lower part of front). Both pants and pullover patterns were lengthened. To calculate how much to lengthen the pants, measure yourself from crotch up to waist, then lengthen so that the curve on the front matches your measurement + seam allowance. As for the top, lengthen the front where the zipper will be by measuring from your front neck to waist; lengthen the top by the same number of inches (centimeters) as missing from your measurements. Cut the back to same length as front. It is better to have too much fabric—and to have to trim away some—than to have too little fabric. We added 1½ in (4 cm) extra in addition to seam allowances. The pockets were lengthened as much as the pants.

Pattern Pieces:

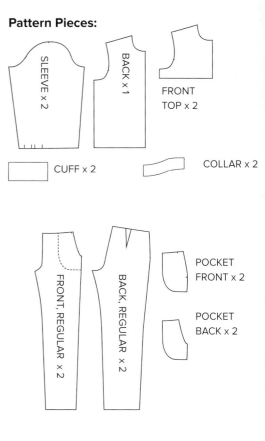

SLEEVE x 2

BACK x 1

FRONT TOP x 2

CUFF x 2

COLLAR x 2

FRONT, REGULAR x 2

BACK, REGULAR x 2

POCKET FRONT x 2

POCKET BACK x 2

1 Cut out all the pieces; iron interfacing to collar and cuffs. Cut strips of interfacing as long and wide as the zippers. Iron on strips where zippers will be placed.

2 Stitch darts on back pieces; follow the line to the original darts and lengthen them at top.

3 Sew front pockets to front with right sides facing. Press seams open and fold pocket to back. Stitch a line along curve ¼ in (0.5 cm) from edge.

4 Place back piece of pocket on front piece and stitch along curve. You can decide if the seam should go through all three layers with a visible seam on the front of the pants or only on the pocket lining. Sew pocket to pants along top edge and on side (stitch inside seam allowance so it won't be visible when the waistband and side seams are joined).

5 Sew side seams and crotch seam on back. The front crotch is not seamed before the pullover and pants are joined.

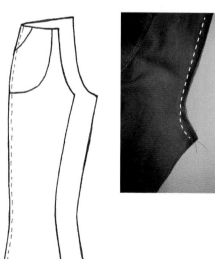

6 Now sew in zippers on front, over chest. They are outside the pocket lining and so can be decorative or for ventilation. If you want to make the jumpsuit without chest pockets, you can skip the next three steps.

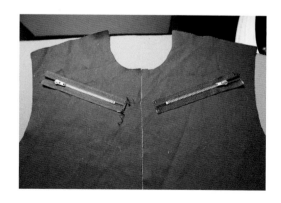

7 Decide where you want to place the chest zippers. Use a ruler to draw a line the same length as zipper.

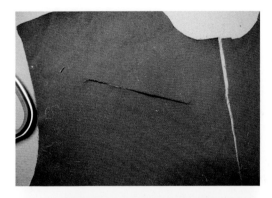

8 Cut along line and cut a small triangle ¼ in (0.5 cm) before the line ends. Fold the triangle and edges back.

9 Place zipper under hole, pin it in place, and then stitch all around it.

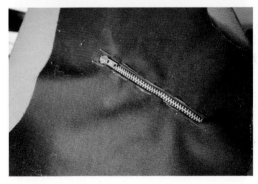

10 Place back and front with right sides facing and seam shoulders.

11 Place collar pieces with right sides facing and stitch together along top curve. Press seams away from each other and, with right sides facing, press.

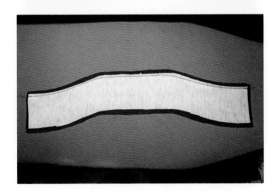

12 Pin and then stitch one side of collar to neck opening, with right sides facing. Press seam toward collar. The rest of the collar is not joined until the zipper is inserted.

If you need to see pictures of these steps, see Sporty Pullover with a Collar.

13 Stitch tucks on lower edges of sleeves following markings on pattern sheet. Sew one long side of cuff to each sleeve with right sides facing. Press seam toward cuff.

15 Fold cuff back to cover seam, press and sew down from right side. Make sure to stitch through all layers.

14 Sew side and sleeve seams from lower edge of pullover to cuff.

16 Try on top and make sure it reaches your waist + ⅜ in (1 cm) seam allowance.

17 The top is wider than the pants, so when you are ready to join them, you can either gather the lower edge of the top or sew with elastic thread (waffle stitching) to draw in the top to fit the pants. We stitched five rows of elastic thread (see page 155 for more details on how to sew waffle stitching, and page 229 for details on gathering).

18 Sew the pants and top together, making sure that the side seams align.

19 Stitch front crotch seam on pants, up to place where zipper will begin.

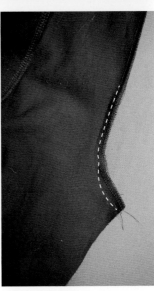

20 Open the zipper and pin it to one front of the top, all the way to the top of the collar. Sew it in firmly. Do the same with the other side of the zipper.

22 Seam between the legs from one leg to the other.

21 Fold raw edges of collar in by ⅜ in (1 cm), press and pin to inside. If you stitch from the right side, you'll have more control for a nicer look. Make sure to stitch through all layers.

23 Hem pant legs by folding up the lower edges and sewing down. You can also fold the hem double.

Jumpsuit from a Dress

Pattern Sheet: Ingrid Pants

Fabric: We made this jumpsuit from a dress. To make a jumpsuit with long legs, you need to start with a dress that is a little too long for you (it can dip in the back). If you have a shorter dress, you can make a jumpsuit with short legs or a shorter length).

Additional Materials: elastic ¾–2 in wide, optional: zipper

Before You Begin: For this pattern, keep the top of the dress. Use the pattern for straight pants, which are lengthened and sewn to the top at the waist. Our dress had a zipper down the back, which we kept as is. If your dress doesn't have a zipper, plan on inserting one.

Pattern Pieces:

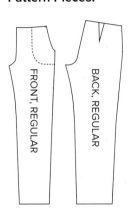

1 Cut out the top a little longer than to your waist.

2 Measure yourself from the center of the crotch up to your waist. Cut out the pants pattern, angling it at the hip line, and shift the pieces far enough from each other so the curve on the front is the same length as your measurement + seam allowance. It is better to add a bit too much for the seam allowance and then trim some away than to have too little fabric. We added 1¼–1½ in (3–4 cm). Place front and back each on its side of side seam. You should cut these in one piece. Add ⅝ in (1.5 cm) seam allowance and cut two pieces that are mirror image. This jumpsuit doesn't have pockets, so the front continues straight up, instead of having a curve cut out for the pocket.

3 Zigzag or overlock all raw edges.

4 Seam front crotch. Pin back crotch seam and make sure you can pull on the pants without a zipper. If yes, sew crotch seam. If not, insert a zipper from back neck and down on the pants.

5 Place pants pieces with right sides facing and seam between the legs.

6 Hem pant legs by folding up the lower edges and sewing down. You can also fold the hem double.

7 Measure the circumference of the lower edge of top and top of pants. If they aren't the same, seam either the top or pants to make it a little narrower, so they will match.

8 Try on top and pants inside out and pin them together with right sides facing. It will be fine if this seam is where waist is smallest. Make sure you can crouch without pants being too tight. Stitch all pieces together. If you have a lot of seam allowance on the inside, trim it and zigzag or overlock edges.

9 Now we'll make the casing and thread the elastic into the waist. Use elastic of width you prefer (mine is 1 in [2.5 cm] wide) and measure it to fit around your waist. Measure the jumpsuit around the waist and cut a band ¾ in (2 cm) longer and 1¼ in (3 cm) wider than the elastic. Zigzag or overlock along the edges. Pin band to inside of jumpsuit at waist. Sew it at top and bottom, leaving an opening at one seamline. Thread elastic through, stitch ends of elastic together, and close opening.

10 Stretch out elastic and stitch through all layers.

11 We made a tie belt with the lining of the dress (see page 232 for details on making a belt).

Jogging Outfit

Pattern Sheet: Ingrid Pants and Ingrid Pullover

Fabric: We made our jogging outfit with curtains from the thrift shop. We also wanted to make the outfit with jersey and wool. Because we held a sewing course at a thrift shop in Bergen, we had permission to choose two things each to take home. Ingrid VL chose these curtains.

Additional Materials: zipper 11–12 in (28–30 cm) long, interfacing, grommets, elastic cord, 5 cord stoppers, 1½ in (4 cm) wide elastic

Before You Begin: The jogging outfit consists of pants and a hooded top. We used the slacks and sporty hooded pullover patterns as our starting point. If you want a baggier outfit, you can go up a size from the one you usually wear.

Pattern Pieces:

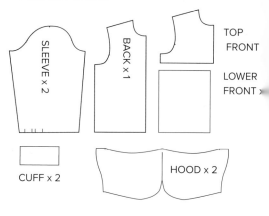

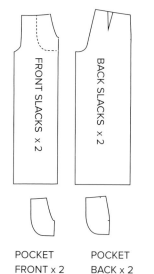

THE PULLOVER TOP:

The hooded top of the jogging outfit is sewn exactly as shown on page 42, but without the pockets. Other adjustments we made are explained below.

The front and back are cut 2¾ in (7 cm) shorter than in the pattern. (If you want a full-length top for the outfit, you can cut out the pattern for the top exactly as is, without shortening it.)

Once you've sewn the top and only need to do the bottom part, work as follows:

1 Fold lower edge 2 in (5 cm) in to wrong side. Mark where you want to place the grommets.

2 Cut out two pieces of interfacing approximately ⅝ × ⅝ in (1.5 × 1.5 cm) and iron them on at markings on wrong side of fabric.

3 Cut a little hole in the fabric where you want each grommet. Place grommet pieces on each side of hole, fasten grommets with grommet tool and secure more firmly with a hammer. The package should have good pictures of how to attach the grommets you have.

4 Stitch casing (the tunnel you made with the folded edge), leaving an opening for inserting elastic.

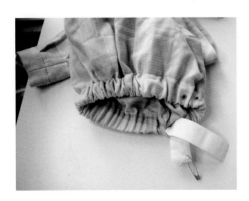

5 Measure the 1½ in (4 cm) wide elastic so it is long enough to go around your waist. It doesn't need to be tight, just to fit comfortably. Attach a safety pin to one end and draw elastic through casing. Seam ends of elastic and then position elastic in casing. Stitch casing opening closed.

6 Cut a piece of elastic cord about 9¾ in (25 cm) longer than waist circumference. Draw cord through casing, out one grommet, though a cord stopper, down in the second grommet, and then through. Tie the ends together and sew the hole in the casing.

PANTS:

The pants are cut following the slacks pattern, with some simple adjustments.

1 From the hip line, cut front and back 90 degrees straight up, but keep the pocket curve on the front pieces. You do not need to mark the darts. Wait to cut out the waistband.

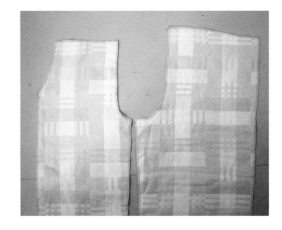

2 Zigzag or overlock around all edges. *Do not stitch* the darts in the pattern.

3 Sew front pockets to front with right sides facing and press seams open. Fold pocket to back and press. Working from right side, stitch along the curve ¼ in (0.5 cm) from edge, through all layers.

4 Place back part of pocket on front and stitch along curve through all three layers for a visible seam on the front. Stitch pockets to pants along top edge and at side (stitch within seam allowance so it won't be visible when the waistband and side seams are sewn).

5 Place front and back with right sides facing and sew side seams on both pant legs.

6 Sew crotch seam on front and back.

7 Sew seams between legs.

8 Measure circumference around waist of pants. Cut a waistband that length + ¾ in (2 cm) and 5½ in (14 cm) wide. Sew waistband into a ring and stitch one edge to pants with right sides facing.

9 Fold waistband so it sags down ⅜ in (1 cm) to front of pants. Pin in place. Attach two grommets on front.

10 Fold waistband to back, over the seam allowance. Pin and then stitch through all three layers. Leave an opening for inserting elastic.

11 Cut elastic cord same length as waist measurement + 13¾ in (35 cm). Draw elastic through waistband, out both grommets, and attach cord stoppers. Knot ends. Measure the 1½ in (4 cm) wide elastic so it is long enough to go around your waist. Attach a safety pin to one end and draw elastic through waistband. Seam ends of elastic and then stitch opening closed.

12 Cut two elastic cords same length as circumference of lower end of pants. Attach a grommet on each side of side seam, 2 in (5 cm) up from edge. Hem legs by folding up edge and stitching down, leaving an opening for elastic. Thread the cords through the grommets and attach cord stoppers. Tie ends of elastic and then stitch opening closed.

SKIRTS AND SHORTS

Welcome to our chapter on skirts and shorts! All the skirts are designed so you can cut out the pieces following your own measurements. We are all different sizes and shapes, and the techniques we use for the skirts mean that they will fit your body perfectly. The shorts are cut following a pattern. We recommend that you take a look at page 12, where you'll find tips on how to adjust a pattern for your body.

The choice of fabric is quite free for these skirts and shorts, and, depending on what kind of fabric you choose, you can make summer or winter garments. The cylinder skirt with a ruffle shown here is made with wool but would be a great summer skirt in a thinner and lighter fabric. A skirt is a garment that doesn't fit the body tightly and might not need to be washed all that often. So, you can make a fine garment with heavy curtains that can't be machine-washed. Any dirt flecks can easily be flicked away with a cloth.

Maxi Skirt

Fabric: Comforter cover with flower pattern

Additional Materials: elastic thread for waffle stitching

Before You Begin: The skirt is cut as a rectangle, so you only stitch a side seam with a split and sew waffle stitching at the waist.

1 Cut a rectangle using your measurements. The length should be as long as you want the skirt to be + ¾ in (2 cm) seam allowance. For the width, your hip measurement × 1.5.

2 Overlock or zigzag all the pieces. Seam the skirt at the side. Make a split beginning at about the middle of your thigh. Make split by ending seam where the split begins. Press seam open from the top all the way down, folding to seam line on split. Stitch split fold.

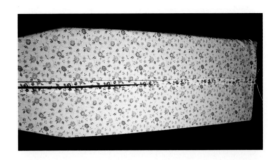

3 Now hem lower edge. Try the skirt on to make sure the length is right and adjust as necessary. Fold up hem on lower edge, press, and then stitch.

4 Prepare top edge of skirt.

5 Work waffle stitching around waist. Waffle stitching is a technique that uses elastic thread as the bobbin thread. When sewn, the fabric gathers evenly, while also making it possible to stretch the fabric back out to full width. First, wind the elastic thread on the bobbin. Machine stitch as usual with the elastic thread on the bottom.

6 Stitch from right side of fabric. Begin by attaching thread to work back and forth.

7 Steam-press waffle stitching so it will compress and gather even more.

Skirt with Elastic Waist

Fabric: We used transparent curtains and lining fabric for our skirt. The skirt can be made with a wide range of fabrics. You can omit the lining if the outer skirt is not transparent.

Additional Materials: 2 in (5 cm) wide elastic

Before You Begin: This skirt can be made with or without a lining. The curtains we used were transparent, so we added a lining. If your fabric isn't transparent, you can make the skirt without a lining. Just follow the instructions, but skip the steps explaining the lining.

1 Cut out the skirt and lining, following the specifications below, and cut a length of elastic long enough to go around your waist + ¾ in (2 cm) seam allowance.

Skirt: Length: your waist measurement + ¾ in (2 cm) seam allowance; width: as long as you want the skirt to be + 2¾ in (7 cm) for casing and seam allowances

Lining: Width: same as for skirt; length: 4 in (10 cm) shorter than skirt

2 Sew side seams on skirt and lining. Fold up lower edges of skirt and lining either once or twice for hem and stitch. We used the curtain's lower edge as the hem for the skirt.

3 Fold down the top edge of the skirt 1½ in (6 cm) to wrong side and press. This forms the casing for the elastic. Place lining ¼ in (0.5 cm) on inside of casing. Pin and stitch all around the skirt, leaving a 1½ in (6 cm) opening so you can thread elastic through casing.

4 Attach a safety pin to one end and draw elastic through casing. Pin and seam ends of elastic. Stitch casing opening closed.

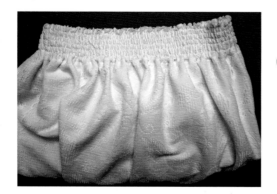

5 Sew five parallel lines along waistband. Pull out elastic as far as it goes while you are sewing to keep fabric straight and so gathers will divide evenly over the whole skirt.

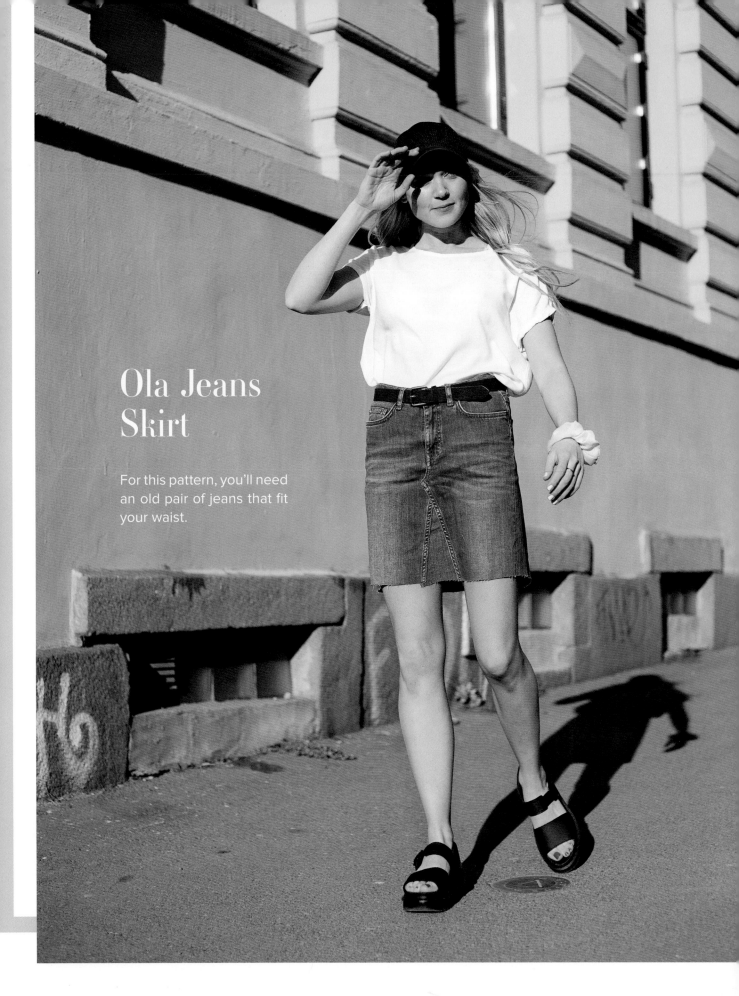

Ola Jeans Skirt

For this pattern, you'll need an old pair of jeans that fit your waist.

1   Cut off jeans to desired
length of skirt.

2   Cut open seams between the legs, all the way to the zipper, beginning at the front and where it curves to the back.

3   Lay pieces flat so they
overlap and make a
triangular opening at
lower edge. Stitch the
overlapping pieces to-
gether by stitching up
the previous seam.

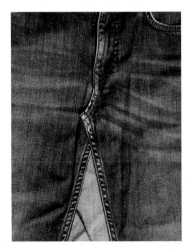

4   Use remaining parts of pants to cut out a bit of fabric larger than the triangular hole. Pin it behind the hole and sew
it along previous seams on jeans.

5   Make the back of the skirt the same way.

Skirt with Flounce

Fabric: We used a heavy wool fabric for our skirt—the leftovers from an Ingrid Jacket we made on our sewing-workshop tour. For a heavier skirt, try firm fabrics, such as a sturdy cotton fabric and curtains, or just wool fabric. We think this skirt works well year-round with leggings underneath.

Additional Materials: 12 in (30 cm) zipper

Before You Begin: This skirt is designed so you can cut out the pieces following your own measurements, so it will fit your body perfectly. Begin with a cylinder, which you can shape to your body with darts, then sew a flounce to lower edge.

1   Measure your hip circumference at widest point. Cut a rectangle that length + ¾ in (2 cm) and as long as you want the skirt to be from your waist to the flounce + ¾ in (2 cm). For example, my (Ingrid VL) rectangle was 36 × 13 in (91 × 33 cm).

2   Cut a band 2.5 times the long side of the rectangle and 6 in (15 cm) in width. If your fabric is thin, multiply by 3, and, if the fabric is extra thick, you can multiply by 2. You might have to splice several pieces of fabric as I did.

3 Zigzag or overlock around all the edges.

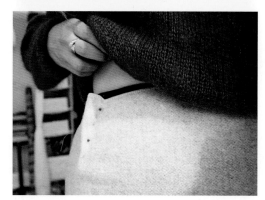

4 Place zipper with right sides facing on short side, ⅜ in (1 cm) below top edge. Using zipper foot on your machine, sew in zipper. Attach the other side the same way. Stitch on each side of zipper from right side to hold it in place.

5 Turn skirt inside out and try on. Fold two darts on front and two on back. A dart is a triangle to bring in fabric and is stitched diagonally down to "nothing" so it looks completely even on the right side. If it seems more natural and more fabric is on the back, you can make two larger darts on the back and omit them on the front. Make sure the darts are placed symmetrically. Stitch and press darts toward the center.

6 Fold the top edge of skirt down ⅜ in (1 cm) and sew down.

7 Now make the flounce. Seam the ends of the band to make a ring. Hem one long side by folding edge up ¼ in (0.5 cm) to wrong side; stitch down.

8 Stitch two gathering lines along the other long side and gather into a circle as big as edge of skirt. Divide gathers evenly and sew gathered edge to skirt with right sides facing. Remove gathering threads (see page 229 for more details on gathering).

Carpenter's Jumper

Fabric: We were lucky to be able to buy this Norwegian-produced fabric from an Instagram follower. We recommend using heavy, firm, tightly woven fabrics. Old jeans certainly work well if you have a few pairs.

Additional Materials: Harness buckle, patent buttons with tools and hammer

Before You Begin: The carpenter's jumper is sewn without a pattern from your own body measurements. You'll need to measure and think a bit geometrically, so we recommend that you sketch an overview on a sheet of paper before you cut out anything. You can also draw the pattern on a pattern sheet so you can save it for later. The jumper/skirt is first cut a bit wide, before you make adjustments for a closer fit. Do not despair if you think it is too wide at first. We did this to avoid a jumper that looks like an apron.

Begin by measuring yourself:

1
- From top of chest to lower edge, and hips to lower edge, to calculate how long the jumper should be
- Hip circumference at widest point
- Top of chest, to calculate width of bib

Now make the front:

2 Divide your hip measurement by two and add 3¼ in (8 cm). This is how wide the front should be on lower part of skirt. Mark this measurement, length, hip length, and width at top of chest. Add 1¼ in (3 cm) in length at the top and make a diagonal line down to the hips. Cut out. This is how I made my front:

10¼ in (26 cm)

Length: 32¼ in (82 cm)

Hip Length: 17¼ in (44 cm)

Width: 21 in (53 cm)

How to make the back:

3 The lower part of the back should be ¾ in (2 cm) wider than the front. Mark this width, the length, and hip length. From the hip length, angle the back over to about the same angle as the front swings in. Continue so that the triangle is 7½ in (19 cm) high. On the back, you can either have the same shaping as the front or do as we did: shift a bit more in (eyeballing it). Cut tip to a very slack tip. This is how I made the back:

Now it's time for sewing:

4 Zigzag or overlock around all edges.

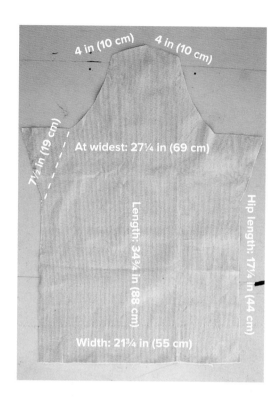

5 Place front and back with right sides facing and seam sides from lower edge to hip.

6 Hem lower edge and edges around front and back by folding in ⅜ in (1 cm) to wrong side; stitch down.

7 Mark and sew three buttonholes on each side of front.

8 Try on jumper and use pins to mark where the buttons will be placed. Attach buttons with tools provided with them and hammer them in.

9 At center front, make two tucks ¼–⅜ in (0.8 cm) in toward center, 1¼ in (3 cm) apart from each other (see page 227 for more details on forming darts). Pin and then top stitch all along tuck.

10 On back, fold down a ⅝ in (1.5 cm) tuck. Stitch two lines along tuck, to hold it in place.

11 Fold down top edge of front 1¼ in (3 cm) to wrong side and sew down.

12 Cut two strips 19¾ in (50 cm) long and same width as buckle + ¾ in (2 cm) (ours were 2 in [5 cm]). Zigzag or overlock. Fold long sides in ⅜ in (1 cm) to wrong side and sew down.

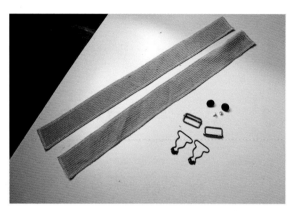 

13 Attach strip to buckle and sew on with adjusting buckle. Fold top edge of back to wrong side, draw straps through underneath and stitch two seams through all layers to hold in place.

14 Attach a button on each side of top front.

Shorts

Pattern Sheet: Ingrid Pants

Fabric: We made our shorts with a flower-strewn curtain.

Additional Materials: regular zipper 8 in (20 cm) long or invisible zipper 9¾ in (25 cm) long

Before You Begin: These shorts are sewn following a pattern completely. You are free to make them shorter or longer so they will suit you perfectly.

Pattern Pieces:

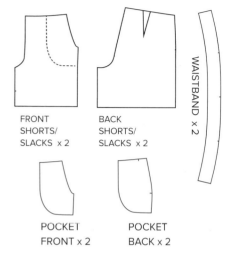

FRONT SHORTS/ SLACKS x 2

BACK SHORTS/ SLACKS x 2

WAISTBAND x 2

POCKET FRONT x 2

POCKET BACK x 2

1   Cut out all pieces and iron interfacing to waistband. Zigzag or overlock around all edges except on waistband.

2   Sew dart on back. (For more details on how to make a dart, see page 227.)

3 Stitch front pocket to front with right sides facing; press seam open. Fold pocket toward back, then press. From front, stitch along curve ¼ in (0.5 cm) from edge, through all layers.

4 Place pocket back on top of front and seam along curve. You can either stitch through all three layers, with stitching visible on front of pants, or only on pocket lining. Sew pocket to pants along top edge and on side (stitch inside seam allowance so it won't be visible when waistband and side seams are sewn).

5 Place front and back with right sides facing and sew side seams on both pant legs.

6 Seam front crotch.

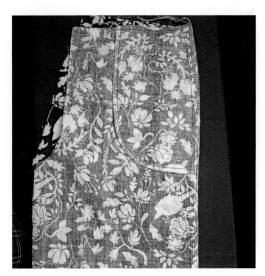

7 Place waistband pieces with right sides facing and seam top edge. Press seam open, fold waistband with wrong sides facing and press.

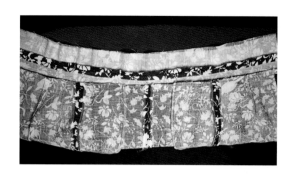

8 Invisible zipper: Insert invisible zipper at center back of pants. Use two pins to mark top of zipper, and place two pins 2 in (5 cm) from lower edge. Pin one side of zipper to pants, all the way up to fold on waistband. Stitch as close to zipper teeth as you can without stitching over them. Stop when you come to the pins marking 2 in (5 cm) from lower edge. Make sure zipper is invisible by closing it. If it is not invisible, you can stitch again, closer to teeth. Pin and then sew in other half of zipper the same way (for how to insert a visible zipper, see page 26).

9 Stitch curve below zipper. Make sure seams meet when zipper closes.

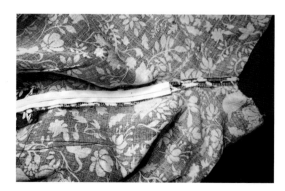

10 Fold in raw edges of waistband ⅜ in (1 cm), press, and pin to inside of pants. If you stitch from the right side, you'll have more control for a nicer look. Make sure to stitch through all layers.

11 Seam between the legs for one leg to the other. Make sure crotch seams meet.

12 Hem pants by folding edge in. You can also make a double fold for hem.

Pattern Pieces:

FRONT
SHORTS/
SLACKS x 2

BACK
SHORTS/
SLACKS x 2

WAISTBAND x 2

POCKET
FRONT x 2

POCKET
BACK x 2

Shorts with Ruffled and Decorated Edgings

These shorts are made the same way as shorts in previous pattern, but with a couple of additions.

Cut out all the pieces as for regular shorts. You'll cut the ruffled edging later, so save a little fabric. To round the lower edge at the sides, use a bowl or plate. Place it 2¾ in (7 cm) from corner. Trace around template with chalk and cut out. Do the same on outer sides of both front and back.

Follow instructions as for shorts until you will hem lower edge.

Measure the circumference around legs, with curve. Cut a band for each leg three times the circumference and 3¼ in (8 cm) wide. If you are sewing with a somewhat heavier fabric, you can use two times the circumference.

Fold band with right sides facing and stitch along long side. Turn, using a safety pin or knitting needle. Press flat. Gather along band and pull in gathers until band matches leg circumference. (For more details on gathering, see page 228.) Sew ruffled band around front of edge. Remove gathering threads.

REDESIGN AND REPAIRS

In this book, most of the garments are made from scratch, using recycled textiles for the fabrics. But you can also make new garments from old clothes. The most difficult parts of the garment are already sewn, which means you can concentrate on simple adjustments to style the garment exactly as you like.

Because the most time-consuming details are already in place, these projects take less time. However, it is important to have a plan before you start cutting, because you only have one chance.

You also need to see what is possible to add or subtract from the garment you have. If, for example, you have a dress with a lot of fabric in it, you will be freer to design whatever you like—something you can't do with a more fitted dress.

If you are redesigning a valuable garment that you are ready to deconstruct, you can add instead of removing something. For example, sew on beads, ribbon, sleeves, or ruffles to spiff up the garment.

The only thing you can't change is the fabric. When you are looking for clothes to redesign, you should keep an eye out for fabrics you like. The fit and design can be changed, but you'll have to live with the fabric. You should also consider the quality of the fabric, making sure you'd like wearing it and that it hasn't become too pilled or worn out.

The magic of redesign is that you can remake old clothes with outdated styling into outfits you can actually wear. Sometimes, you'll need to make only small changes, but other times, you can remake a garment into something totally different.

From a Suit to a Dressy Jacket and Pants

This suit was a recycling coup from a thrift store. Ingrid VL and I hold redesigning workshops where we each pick out a starting garment. I immediately fell for the fabric and dress jacket and could see that the dress had enough fabric to make into a skirt and top or pants.

I decided to make pants with the dress and to keep the jacket as is. To make the pants, I began with the pants pattern in this book. Since the dress didn't have enough fabric to make full-length pants, I made them as long as possible.

I left the side zipper in the dress and cut the front and back so I could avoid sewing side seams later.

Pattern Pieces:

FRONT, REGULAR x 2

BACK, REGULAR x 2

WAISTBAND x 2

From an '80s Outfit to a Dress

I inherited this outfit from a friend of my mother's. She bought it in the 1980s, totally falling for the bright colors. She wore it for a number of years, but then it hung in the closet.

The fabric is gorgeous, but the styling is very old-fashioned. Since the skirt has so much fabric, I could use it as yardage (meterage) and make something completely different. I liked the puff sleeves and buttons on the front and wanted to keep as much fabric as possible. So, I removed the vest from the jacket and sewed the skirt and top into a dress. I folded in the black wool lower edging on the skirt to retain the weight of the skirt. I sewed casings at each side of the skirt and inserted tie cords so I could pull up the hem to make a split at each side for a more bubble skirt look.

Front Tie Top

A super-easy redesign, where the only thing you have to do is cut the top so you can tie it. You do have to use a fabric that won't unravel; we used jersey tops.

1   Try on top and use a pin to mark where you want the front knot.

2   Cut a straight line up to the pin.

3   Knot top. If you pull a little on the fabric, the edges will roll together nicely.

Pullover with Side Ties

This trick can be used for any garments that are too long, or to spice up a garment. You can sew casings on pant legs, on sleeves, or at the sides of a pullover, which we've done here. You'll need fabric and cords.

1 Measure the side of the top, from underarm seam down.

2 Cut two bands that length and 1½ in (4 cm) wide.

3 Pin bands along side seams on inside of top.

4 Center each band on side seam and stitch down center and ⅜ in (1 cm) out on each side of seam, so you have three parallel stitching lines and two casings.

5 Cut two cords at least twice as long as the side seam. Knot cord ends or melt with a lighter. Attach a safety pin on the cord end and draw cord up through one casing and down through the other at each side.

Repairing with Embroidery

We all experience holes in our garments from time to time. It's not very environmentally friendly to simply discard or repurpose a garment because of a little hole. A hole can offer a good opportunity to make a unique garment: you can embroider over the hole.

Ingrid VL bought a shirt in a used-clothing shop, but when she got home, she discovered that it had two small holes. It was lucky that it took her a while before she repaired the shirt, because then we could use it for this book!

You'll need interfacing, an embroidery needle, and embroidery thread or yarn. You can use as many of the thread strands as you wish to create the thinness or thickness you prefer. If you are unsure, you can sample on a swatch first.

1 Cut out a circle of interfacing a bit larger than the hole. Iron onto back of hole.

2 Knot one end of thread. Attach thread on back of fabric. Embroider as you like. The internet is full of inspiration. We embroidered on two daisies.

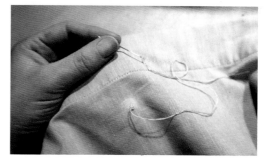

Repairing with Beads

This top also had a few small holes—we showed how to embroider over them on the previous page. In this case, we repaired the holes by stitching over them and then sewed beads all around the neckline.

Holes in Your Jeans

It is really annoying when you get rips and tears in your favorite jeans or pants. Luckily, these are easier to fix than you might think, and the results are invisible if you find some thread that matches the color of the pants.

1 Cut out a piece of interfacing or fabric a little larger than the hole. Pin the piece behind the hole (iron on if using interfacing).

2 Stitch back and forth in straight lines over the hole in several directions.

3 This photo shows the hole completely covered over. The closer the thread color matches that of the garment, the more invisible the repair will be. In addition, the fabric will be stronger where you repaired it.

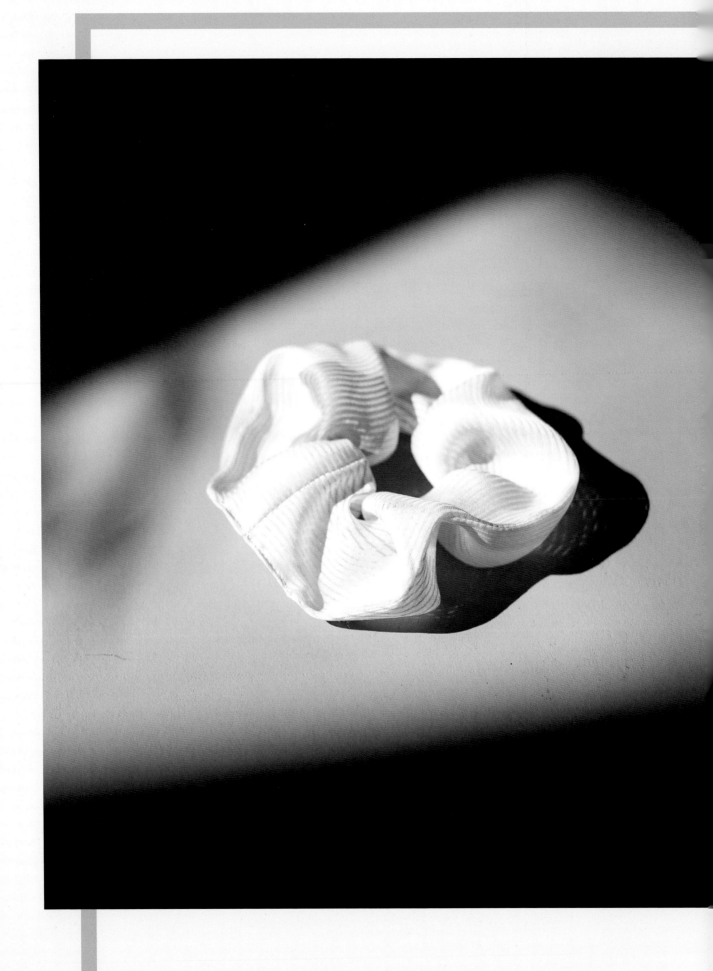

FABRIC REMNANTS

When you sew, you can hardly avoid having fabric remnants. Sometimes, the leftovers are tiny and it is difficult to sew anything from them. Some can be saved and used as filling in a cushion or teddy bear. Somewhat larger pieces are easier to sew with. To get the best possible use of textiles, it's a good idea to have a few patterns for remnants in the back of your mind. That way, you keep fabrics from becoming waste and, at the same time, can make some terrific items. We collected a few patterns perfect for remnants here. Some use small pieces; others need larger pieces. These items are great as gifts. If you have some fabric left over after a project, you can, for example, make scrunchies with it all and give them away.

Caps

Fabric: You make a cap with tightly woven fabrics. Since you'll iron interfacing on the back of the fabric, you can also use a thinner fabric. A wool cap or heavier upholstery is fine for fall or spring, but caps made from embroidered cloth are super sweet for summer.

Additional Materials: an old cap, interfacing, ⅜ in (1 cm) wide elastic

Before You Begin: The cap is made by separating all the pieces of an old cap. The brim and the soft padding on the inside will be widened, while the other pieces are used as a template to make new pieces in your chosen fabric. Look carefully at your cap and take some pictures of how it was sewn together before you deconstruct it.

1 Separate the cap. In the cap itself, there are often four similar pieces (shaped like pizza slices) and two similar pieces on the back. Be careful with the brim and soft padding along the inner edge, but separate the fabric above it.

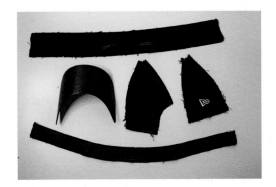

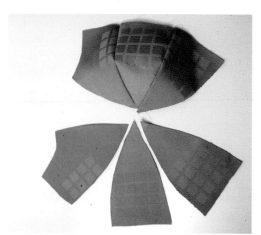

2 Iron the pieces flat. Lay them on your fabric and cut out new pieces.

3 Iron interfacing onto all the cap pieces. With right sides facing, stitch the pieces together. It is important that you keep the same size seam allowances as on the original cap. Press seams open before you stitch the two back pieces together.

4 Try cap on. If it is too big, you can re-stitch the seams closer in.

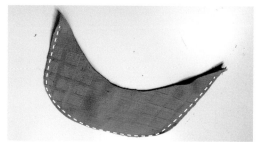

5 With right sides facing, sew brim pieces together along curve. Notch seam allowance and turn. Push brim in, tighten fabric around it and pin. Change to zipper foot on your machine and stitch as close as possible to the brim.

6 Measure to center of brim and pin brim and cap with right sides facing. Sew securely by hand or with the zipper foot on your sewing machine, as close to the brim as possible. (We machine-stitched to this point and then sewed the rest of the cap by hand.)

7 Fold a fabric strip around the padding and stitch along each edge to keep it in place.

8 Sew the padded band to the cap with wrong side facing right side. (We machine-stitched along the sides and sewed along the brim by hand.)

9 Fold the padded band out of the cap and place it over the entire edge of back opening by folding ⅜ in (1 cm) in to wrong side; stitch in place.

10 Now make the elastic band to hold the cap together at the back. Try on cap and measure for length of elastic. Cut a piece of fabric 1½ × 6¼ in (4 × 16 cm). Fold fabric strip with right sides facing and stitch along long side; turn right side out and press. Insert elastic into casing. Stitch it to padding. Tack by hand if necessary.

11 Sew bias tape over seams by hand.

Bucket Hat

Pattern Sheet: Ingrid Hat / Ingrid Skirt

Fabric: We made our bucket hat with a flowered bed sheet and remnants from the maxi skirt

Additional Materials: interfacing

Before You Begin: The bucket hat is lined—you make two identical hats, with one side as a lining and the other as the outer shell fabric. You can decide if you want to make the entire cap with one fabric or use something else for the lining. If you choose two different fabrics, they should be about the same weight.

Pattern Pieces:

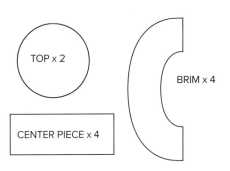

1 Cut out all the pieces and iron interfacing on any thin fabric pieces. (We ironed interfacing onto all the pieces.)

2 Stitch brim together and the two side pieces on side seams.

3 Pin and sew top of hat to side pieces; press.

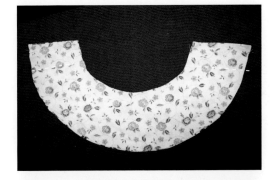

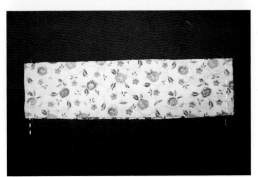

4 Pin and stitch brim to other side of side pieces; press.

5 Place the two hats with right sides facing. Make sure the side seams align, and stitch along the outer edge of the brim. Leave a large enough opening so you can pull the hat through.

6 Turn hat right side out and steam-press it well.

7 Stitch parallel lines along brim, spaced ¼ in (0.5 cm) apart.

Scrunchie

Fabric: For this pattern, we used a shawl Ingrid B inherited from her grand-mother. It had a tear in it, so it was perfect for the new life we could give it as a scrunchie.

Additional Materials: elastic ¼ in (0.5 cm) wide

Before You Begin: This pattern is for a scrunchie that is a bit large. If you want a narrower one or one with more ruffles, you can cut out a narrower, longer rect-angle. Use fabric you have on hand as a starting point for the design.

1 Cut out a rectangle 6 in (15 cm) wide and 15¾ in (40 cm) long.

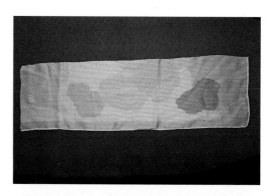

2 Double the fabric and stitch along top edge. Begin and end 1½ in (4 cm) from each end.

3 Press seam open; turn right side out.

4 Lay ends with right sides facing and stitch together. To get all the way around, you'll have to move the fabric as you stitch while the needle is down. Make sure piece stays flat as you sew.

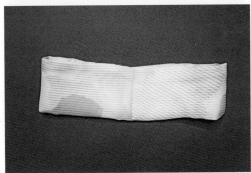

5 Fold seam to inside and press all around.

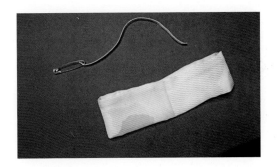

6 Cut a piece of elastic 8 in (20 cm) long. Attach a safety pin to one end and draw through opening. Tie elastic ends and hide them in scrunchie.

7 Stitch along edge to close the hole.

Makeup Pads

Makeup pads do not need to be single-use only. These can be washed and reused. Another advantage is that they are small and perfect for using up soft fabric scraps, old hand towels, or cloths. Our makeup pads are two sided. On one side we used an old cloth, and on the other, jersey fabric scraps.

1 Draw and cut out a paper template in the size you like. We just placed a glass upside down and traced around it.

2 Place the template on the fabric and draw around it with chalk. Cut out as the same number of pieces in each fabric.

3 Place pieces on each other with wrong sides facing. Pin in the middle so they won't slide. Zigzag or overlock around all edges. If you zigzag, make a sample first. We recommend wide stitches with a short stitch length, so the edge will stay well within the seam.

BAGS

In this chapter, we'll show you how to make your own bags. For the best possible results, we recommend heavy, tightly woven fabric, such as denim, leather, or sturdy cotton. Bags are often constructed of several small pieces sewn together, which means that you can use garments as yardage (meterage) for cutting out pieces from each other. This is great if you have a torn leather jacket or jeans you want to give new life to.

Coin Purse

Fabric: We used an old leather skirt from a flea market. The zipper was rusty and the leather torn in several places. The lining had begun to sag, so we decided to revive it as something completely different.

Additional Materials: zipper 8 in (20 cm)

Before You Begin: Since we were sewing with leather, we kept the edges of the fabric exactly as they were. If you are sewing with fabric that unravels, follow the steps indicated.

1 Cut a rectangle 8¼ × 12¾ in (21 × 32 cm). *For fabric that unravels: Zigzag or overlock around all edges.*

2 Place zipper on fabric with right side facing wrong side. Change to zipper foot on machine and stitch in zipper. Before you run into zipper bottom, stop, lift foot and pull retaining box underneath it. Stitch zipper to opposite side the same way. *For fabric that unravels: Place zipper with right sides facing before you stitch it in, so the edge of the fabric will be on the inside when you are finished.*

3 Turn so fabric lies with right sides facing and zipper is on top. Stitch along sides of zipper again, down to the stop.

4 Turn right side out and push out corners.

Bag

Fabric: Thick, closely woven fabrics are best for this bag—denim, leather, or sturdy cotton. The bag is sewn with the same skirt as used for the coin purse: an old leather skirt from a flea market.

Additional Materials: zipper 12 in (30 cm), two carbine hooks, chain link or another type of strap, paper

Before You Begin: Since we were sewing with leather, we kept the edges of the fabric exactly as they were. If you are sewing with fabric that unravels, follow the steps indicated. Our bag is constructed of two rectangular, rounded-edge side pieces; a base; two top pieces with a zipper in between; an attachment for the strap; and a chain-link strap. You can decide on the bag's size, but we will give you a starting point. Before you cut out the fabric pieces, make paper pattern templates.

1 Begin by drawing paper pattern templates:

- Side pieces: Cut two rectangles 6¼ × 8¼ in (16 × 21 cm) and round the corners.
- Top pieces: Cut two rectangles 12¾ × 2½ in (32 × 6.5 cm).
- Base: Measure the circumference around the side piece. Subtract 11 in (28 cm) and cut a rectangle with this measurement as the length and 2½ in (6.5 cm) wide.

2 Cut all the pieces in fabric.
For fabric that unravels: Zigzag or overlock around all edges.

3 Insert zipper between the two top pieces. Pin zipper with right sides facing along one top piece. Change to zipper foot on machine and stitch in zipper. About ¼ in (0.5 cm) of the zipper tape at the stop will be visible. Stitch other top piece to other side of zipper. From the right side, stitch along other side of the zipper to hold seam allowance in place.

4 Stitch base and top pieces along short sides with right sides facing. Leave a little hole about ¾ in (2 cm) at zipper stop—you'll sew on a little loop here for attaching the carbine hooks later.

5 Pin and then stitch side pieces with right sides facing.

6 Cut two pieces of fabric ¾ × 2 in (2 × 5 cm). Fold fabric lengthwise with wrong sides facing and seam along edge.
For fabric that unravels: Cut fabric 1¼ × 2 in (3 × 5 cm). Fold fabric with wrong sides facing and then fold in raw edges. Press and seam along edge.

7 Draw fabric piece through carbine hooks and push edge down through opening below zipper. Stitch through all layers to secure them. Measure the chain link and clip to carbine hooks.

Tote Bag

Fabric: This tote bag is sewn with an imitation leather. For a style more in line with shopping, you can make the bag with cotton. All patterns and colors are workable, but make sure the fabric is sturdy so it won't sag down your back when you're carrying something heavy.

Before You Begin: The tote bag consists of a rectangular piece of fabric. The base is made by sewing the corners. If you want a larger or smaller bag than ours, you can measure up or down to scale. Since our bag was made with faux leather and the edges won't unravel, the process is a little different. This method also works for leather, wool blanket fabric, plastic, and other fabrics that won't unravel along the edges. If you are sewing with fabric that does unravel on the edge, follow the steps indicated.

1 Cut out:

- a rectangle 17¾ × 35½ in (45 × 90 cm)
- two strips 1½ × 28¼ in / 2½ × 28¼ in (4 × 72 cm) / (6 × 72 cm)
- one square 7 × 7 in (18 × 18 cm)

For fabric that unravels: Zigzag or overlock around all edges on rectangle and square.

2 Fold rectangle with right sides facing and stitch along the two sides.

3 *For fabric that unravels: Fold strips lengthwise with right sides facing. Stitch along long side. Use a chopstick or safety pin to turn the strips right side out. Press flat so seam is on the underside.*

4 Fold top edge of bag 2 in (5 cm) down to wrong side and press. Push ends of strap in under fold, 3½ in (9 cm) from each side, and pin.

5 On right side, stitch a square to attach straps, then stitch folded edge down.

6 Fold straps with wrong sides facing and seam. This does not apply to fabrics that can unravel.

7 Stitch one edge of pocket down to wrong side.

8 Pin pocket on inside of bag and stitch along all sides except the top one.

For fabric that unravels: Before you sew on the pocket, fold and press the other edges, pin pocket to inside of bag, and stitch along these three sides.

9 Fold out corners on base of bag so side seam is centered on triangle. Stitch 2½ in (6.5 cm) from top of triangle. If you want a wider or narrower base, make seam farther from or nearer top. We recommend that you place pins where the seam will be, and try out the bag before you stitch.

Fanny Pack

Fabric: Wool as well as embroidered cloth for lining

Additional Materials: zippers 6 in (15 cm), 7 in (18 cm), 8 in (20 cm), and 10 in (25 cm); interfacing; adjusting buckle, and fastening buckle to close belt; bias tape

Before You Begin: This is the most advanced pattern in our book because there are so many pieces, zippers, bias tape, and a lining. The fanny pack is constructed with a main section and two inner pockets, plus a little pocket on the front. The little pocket has a zipper at center front and on the top, both on the same pocket. You can make it easier by omitting some of the pockets if you want.

The outer fabric for the fanny pack has eight pieces, while the lining has eleven. Cut out the pieces following these measurements.

Outer Fabric

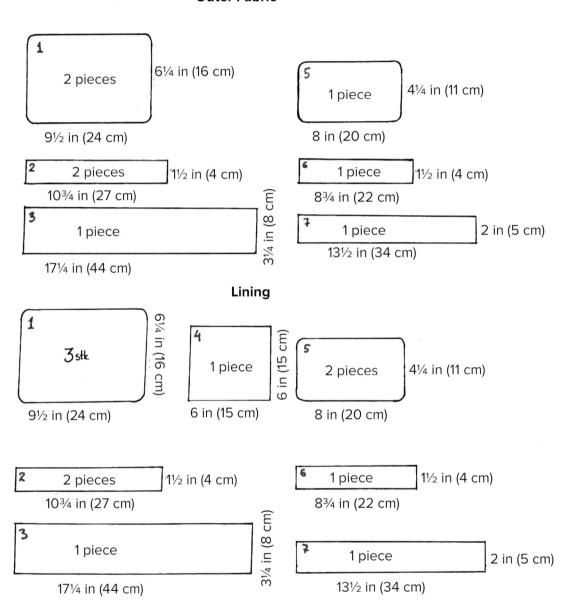

The numbers in red indicate the pattern piece number as referenced in the instructions.

1 Cut out all the pieces, then iron interfacing onto any outer fabric pieces that need to be stiffened.

The small outer pocket:

2 Place 7 in (18 cm) zipper on top of piece 5 (outer fabric). Decide on placement of zipper and cut piece 5 in two where the zipper will be inserted. (We cut it in two about 1¼ in [3 cm] from the top.) Cut lining in same place.

3 Place zipper between lining and outer fabric, pin and then stitch together. Fold lining and outer fabric back, press, and stitch along seam. Do the same on the fabric above zipper.

4 Place 8 in (20 cm) zipper between lining and outer fabric, piece 6. Sew them together along top edge, fold lining and fabric back, press, and stitch along seam.

5

Place lining and outer fabric piece 7 on each side of short end where zipper ends, pin, press and stitch. This long piece is the side around the outer pocket of the fanny pack.

6

Place short sides with right sides facing on each side of zipper and sew sides into a circle. Fold back, press, and stitch.

7

Now the two pieces are joined. Pin the base and sides together and sew all around.

Before joining small pocket to bag, sew on pockets and loops for belt at waist.

8 Begin with piece 4, the small pocket inside the bag. Fold the top side ⅜ in (1 cm) back, press and seam to hold in place. Press the other three sides ⅜ in (1 cm) back. Place pocket centered on lining piece 1. Stitch it along the three sides pressed in. Place fabric piece with pocket on outer fabric piece 1, with wrong sides facing so pocket points out on one side and the right side of outer fabric on the other. Stitch them together all around, ¼ in (0.5 cm) from edge.

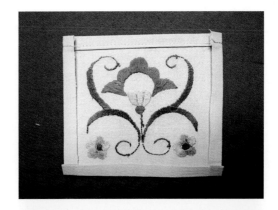

9 Cut off two strips of belt about 2½ in (6 cm); melt or sew sides before you sew it to piece 1 (outer fabric). Check the space between the two seams with a little bit of the belt to make sure that it can be drawn through later on.

10

To make the pockets with zippers on the inside of the pack, cut lining piece 1 in two where you want to insert the zipper. We used a 6 in (15 cm) zipper and cut two extra squares of lining fabric to fill in the extra space missing on each side of the zipper. Sew the squares on each side of the zipper, press, and tack down. Do the same with the top piece. Place pocket on the other lining piece and sew them together all around, ¼ in (0.5 cm) from edge.

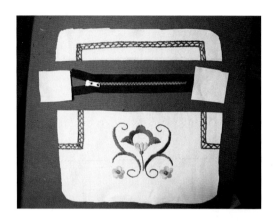

11

Place lining pieces with zipper pocket and outer fabric where belt will be attached on top of each other with wrong sides facing and stitch together all around, ¼ in (0.5 cm) from edge.

12

Place piece 2 (lining and outer fabric) on each side of the 10 in (25 cm) zipper. Stitch along top edge. Do the same on both sides of the zipper, press and top stitch.

13

Place piece 3 (lining and outer fabric) on each side of short end where zipper ends, pin and stitch into place.

14

Place short sides with right sides facing on each side of zipper and stitch sides into a ring. Fold back, press, and top stitch.

15

Stitch sides and back of bag together all around.

Finally, join all the parts of bag.

To hide the raw edges and prevent them from unraveling, we sewed bias tape along all raw edges inside the bag. You can either make the bias tape yourself or buy it, as we did here. On page 230, you'll find information about how to make and sew on bias tape.

16 Turn small pocket so lining faces out. Trim seam allowance to about ¼ in (0.5 cm) and sew on bias tape. Sew bias tape along the outermost edge also. Now the outer pocket is completely ready to be attached to the fanny pack. To attach pocket, iron on bias tape, place outer pocket on outer fabric piece 1, pin and sew on from right side. After outer pocket is attached to outer fabric, sew lining piece 1 to outer fabric with wrong sides facing, approximately ¼ in (0.5 cm) from edge all around.

17 Trim seam allowance on inside of main pocket in bag, pin and sew bias tape along all raw edges.

18 Pin and sew front of pack to sides, all around. Make sure that zipper top is a little open when you sew, so you can open and turn the bag after it has been stitched together.

19 Trim seam allowance and sew bias tape along all raw edges.

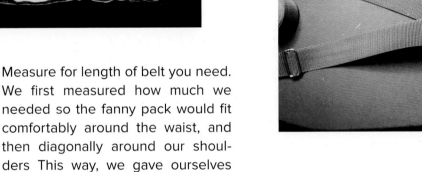

20 Measure for length of belt you need. We first measured how much we needed so the fanny pack would fit comfortably around the waist, and then diagonally around our shoulders This way, we gave ourselves options for how to use it.

21 Draw adjusting buckles onto belt, and then the one attachment buckle; bring end of belt back through adjusting buckle and stitch down.

TECHNIQUES

Throughout the book, some techniques are repeated. For example, gathering is used to make puff sleeves, but also several dresses and cuffs are gathered. If you've already learned this technique, you don't need a long explanation every time. We gathered some of the most important techniques here—so you can come back to them as needed.

Darts and Tucks

DARTS

A dart is used to form or shape a garment, such as, for example, on the back of pants or toward the breasts on a top. On the pants pattern in this book, we have two darts, one on each part of the back. It is marked on the pattern sheet with two triangles beginning at the top of the back piece.

When cutting out fabric, the darts should be marked with chalk or pins. You sew a dart by folding the triangle in half so the fabric lies with right sides facing; stitch along the marking. Press the dart toward center of garment.

TUCKS

A tuck is a fold in the fabric that shapes in the same way as darts, but a tuck is sewn only along the edge of the fabric. In both shirt and top patterns in this book, we added tucks in the sleeves above the cuffs. They are marked as a square with an arrow on the pattern sheets.

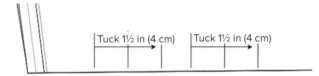

Tuck 1½ in (4 cm)   Tuck 1½ in (4 cm)

The cargo pants have two tucks facing each other on the pocket.

Mark tucks with chalk or pins when you cut out the pattern. Sew tucks by folding the fabric over in the direction indicated by the arrow, so the fabric aligns edge to edge on each side of tuck. Stitch along the top edge to hold the tuck in place.

Gathers

HOW TO GATHER FABRIC:

Step 1: Change the setting on your sewing machine to a maximum stitch length of ⅛–¼ in (4 or 5 mm) and set thread tension to 1. Change top thread and bobbin thread to a color that contrasts well with the fabric you are sewing with. This makes it easier to see which are gathering threads and which aren't.

Step 2: Pull out about 4 in (10 cm) of top and bobbin threads before beginning to sew. Stitch along edge of fabric without securing thread. Keep sewing machine foot edge to edge with the fabric so you know you are stitching in a straight line. When you get to the end of the fabric, do not secure thread but pull out about 4 in (10 cm) of top and bobbin threads. Stitch another line as before, about ¼ in (0.5 cm) below first line.

Step 3: From right side of fabric, insert a pin centered between the two gathering threads, and wrap the two top threads in a figure eight around the pin. Let the two bobbin threads hang loose. Do the same at both ends.

Step 4: Pull on the two bobbin threads at the same time as pulling the fabric inward, so you can see that it is gathering. Try to distribute the gathers as evenly as possible along the fabric.

Step 5: Pin the gathered fabric to the fabric piece it will join, and stitch between the two gathering threads. Don't forget to change back to your working thread color and to change the setting on the machine for the normal stitch length. Remove gathering threads.

Bias Tape

Bias tape is a narrow strip of fabric cut on the diagonal, folded single or double and used mainly for finishing or as an embellishment on a garment.

Bias tape is a super method of finishing edges on a garment. It is called bias tape because it is cut on the diagonal to give the band elasticity and flexibility to stitch along both curved and straight edges. If you learn how to make you own bias tape, you can make the bands in the same fabric as the garment.

HOW TO MAKE BIAS TAPE:

You'll need a tool for folding bias tape. Bias tape makers come in various sizes, and the size determines how wide of a fabric strip you can cut. Here, we used a bias tape maker to make a fabric strip 1½ in (3.8 cm). The ends of the band should be cut on the diagonal so it will be easy to feed strips into the bias tape maker.

Often, one doesn't have enough remnants to cut the whole length of the band. In that case, it is necessary to splice several pieces together. Splice the band as shown here:

HOW TO SEW A BIAS TAPE:

Step 1: Draw strip through bias tape maker. Press the fabric as it comes out folded from the end of the maker.

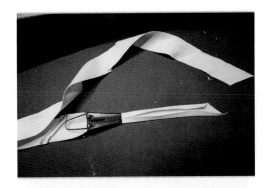

Step 2: Roll the tape up as you make more and more, until all the band is folded.

Step 3: Fold back the end of the bias tape ¼ in (0.5 cm) and pin one side of the bias tape in the garment, with right sides facing, all around the opening. Stitch along fold.

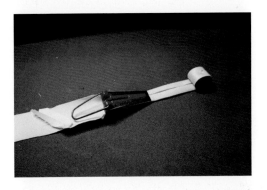

Step 4: Fold the bias tape over the edge, press and pin down. Stitch from right side of fabric along lower edge of bias tape, making sure seam goes through all fabric layers.

Tie Belt

A belt to tie around your waist is a great way to shape a silhouette or just to dress up a garment. We made belts for several garments in this book.

To determine how long to make the belt, tie a long band, rope, or measuring tape around your waist to fit as you want. Measure the length of this band. If you want a very wide belt, over 4 in (10 cm), you should add a bit extra to the length, since the loop "points" more of the length on a side belt.

Cut the fabric strips to measured length and width (twice the width you want for the belt + ¾ in (2 cm). You can splice several pieces if the fabric is not large enough. Fold the band lengthwise and trim corners so the ends are pointed.

Fold strip lengthwise, with right sides facing. Stitch along the long side and the two short ends, leaving an opening at the center.

Opening

Trim corners at points and pull belt through opening using a chopstick or safety pin.

Press belt flat and stitch opening closed.

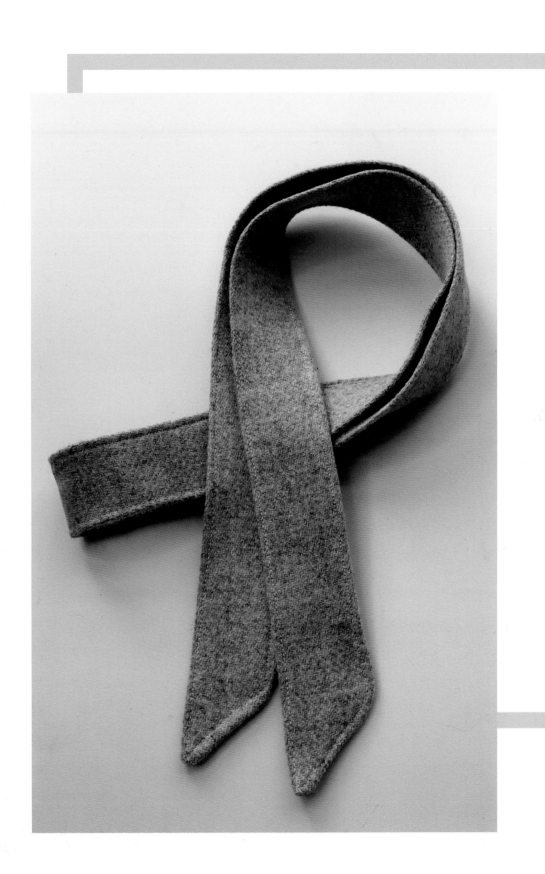

Our Test Sewists

As we worked on this book, we needed to test the fit of the patterns in various sizes, so we asked our followers on Instagram if anyone wanted to test sew our patterns and give feedback on sizing and fit, and to let us know of any errors that needed to be corrected. More than 500 people volunteered to sew for us, totally unbelievable and unexpected. At random, we chose 150 people of different sizes, and received a huge amount of valuable feedback, which we used to make our instructions and patterns even better. We couldn't have done it without you! Thank you ever so much. You are gold!

Amalie Holen @amalie.holen

Amina Louragli @fashion.by.amina

Ann Helen Paulsen @frkpaulsen

Nora Landmark-Rosen

@julestheunicorn

@idunnogvanebo

Rakel Heggelund @rakeellh

Therese Fjæra Almås @theresealmaas

@henrietteharbo

Ingvill @ingvillsyr

Ane-Marthe Skredderstuen @skreddersystuen

Frida Vestby @fruvestby

Eirin Aspenes Wold @eirin

Ellen-Andrea

Bianca M Alvestad @lifes_sweet_moments

Hanne Stakkestad

Hedda Kilen @heddakilen

Hedda Marie Bay @heddabay

Heidi Marie Helgerud

Hermine @Herminesyr

Ida Bergheim Dalene @ldabergheimdalene

Idunn Mostue @idunnaam

Nanna Myhre @nannajinshao

Mari Heggernes Eilertsen @hobbymari

Maria Grenda Andersson @bohemsko

Moa Bodemar @moa_syr.no

Monica Foss @frumonicafoss

Ine Alheim-Blyberg @inealheim

Inger Kristine Stusdal Alfsvåg @ika_syr

Inger Petina Skavdal @ingerpetina

Jessica @lou.earthflower

Kaja Bestvold @bestvoldstrikk

Karoline Sørensen @kreakaro

Karoline @petit.karol

Katrine Kjenne @katrinesyr

Kristina Cronfelt Aasen @Kristinacron

Kristine Grønningsæter @sykluss

Kristine Gundersen @gundersen.kristine

Kristin Talleraas @kristin.talleraas

Kristin Norrmann @kristinnorm

Linda Aannø @a.a.n.n.o

Line Mølle-Stray Nissen @linemsnissen

Linn Alnes Djuvsland @Kreativlinn

Lovise Aufles Valberg @valbergdesign

Magdalena Simma @lenisprojects

Malin Hovde @syfrk

Margrethe Oma @made.by.milli

Maria Warpe

Marie Hansen @stoffavhengig

Marina Sariberget @msariberget

Marthe Klovning Flem @m.k.creates

Marthe Wensaas @marthewe

Merete Moe @handverksfrua

Michelle Bratt @michelle.sbn

Ole Martin Sandland @olesandland

Ragnhild Tuften @ragnhildtuften

Ragnhild Zachariassen @fruzach

Rose Marie Jonassen @rosemj_syr

Sidsel Skjøde @sidselskjoede

Signe Stølan Høgberg @siggisnuppa

Silje Marie Øyen @siljeoyensyr

Silje Storebø @Siljesyr

Silje Helene Knudsen @Siljeksyr

Silje Sletta Strand @hverdags_inspirasjon

Sine Alise Hansen @sinealise

Siri Lindsveen @sirilindsveensyr

Siri Sørlie Jørgensen
@siriipirii

William Waardal
@william.waardal

Yvonne Seem
@fruseemsyr

Elisabeth Bartnes Sylten
@frkbartnes

OTHER SCHIFFER BOOKS ON RELATED SUBJECTS:

Upcycle Your Wardrobe: 21 Sewing Projects for Unique, New Fashions, Mia Führer, ISBN 978-0-7643-4849-5

The Little Guide to Mastering Your Sewing Machine: All the Sewing Basics, Plus 15 Step-by-Step Projects, Sylvie Blondeau, ISBN 978-0-7643-4970-6

Artisan Felting: Wearable Art, Jenny Hill, ISBN 978-0-7643-5852-4

Cover design by Ashley Millhouse
Interior design by Terese Moe Leiner
Pattern sheets: Mari Nordén

Type set in Proxima Nova

ISBN: 978-0-7643-6613-0
Printed in China

Published by Schiffer Publishing, Ltd.
4880 Lower Valley Road
Atglen, PA 19310
Phone: (610) 593-1777; Fax: (610) 593-2002
Email: Info@schifferbooks.com
Web: www.schifferbooks.com

For our complete selection of fine books on this and related subjects, please visit our website at www.schifferbooks.com. You may also write for a free catalog.

Schiffer Publishing's titles are available at special discounts for bulk purchases for sales promotions or premiums. Special editions, including personalized covers, corporate imprints, and excerpts, can be created in large quantities for special needs. For more information, contact the publisher.

We are always looking for people to write books on new and related subjects. If you have an idea for a book, please contact us at proposals@schifferbooks.com.

Photos:
Anna Torst Saatvedt: pages 3–5, 8, 21, 24–25, 27, 29–30, 33, 36, 38, 43, 45, 49, 54, 57, 62–65, 68, 71, 76, 80, 87, 96, 102, 110, 114, 116, 121, 132, 135, 140, 145, 151–152, 154, 156, 159, 161, 164, 169, 174, 176, 179–180, 183–184, 187–188, 190, 192, 196, 199, 202, 204, 208, 211–212, 216
Ingrid Bergtun and Ingrid Vik Lysne: pages 22, 23, 26, 28, 29 (*top*), 34, 35, 37, 39–42, 46–48, 50–53, 56, 58–61, 66–67, 70, 72–74, 77–79, 81–95, 86, 88–89, 91–94, 97–101, 103–109, 111–113, 117–120, 122–124, 125–131, 134, 136–139, 141–144, 147–150, 155, 157–158, 160, 162–163, 165–168, 170–173, 175, 178, 181–182, 185–186, 189, 193–195, 197–198, 200–201, 203, 207, 209–210, 213, 218–220, 232
Joachim Stenbru: pages 90–95
All photos on pages 234–239 used with permission